PLATO (c.427–347 BCE), Athenian philosopher-dramatist, has had a profound and lasting influence upon Western intellectual tradition. Born into a wealthy and prominent family, he grew up during the conflict between Athens and the Peloponnesian states which engulfed the Greek world from 431 to 404 BCE. Following its turbulent aftermath, he was deeply affected by the condemnation and execution of his revered master Socrates (469–399) on charges of irreligion and corrupting the young. In revulsion from political activity, Plato devoted his life to the pursuit of philosophy and to composing memoirs of Socratic enquiry cast in dialogue form. He was strongly influenced by the Pythagorean thinkers of southern Italy and Sicily, which he is said to have visited when he was about 40. Some time after returning to Athens, he founded the Academy, an early ancestor of the modern university, devoted to philosophical and mathematical enquiry, and to the education of future rulers or 'philosopher-kings'. The Academy's most celebrated member was the young Aristotle (384–322), who studied there for the last twenty years of Plato's life. Their works mark the highest peak of philosophical achievement in antiquity, and both continue to rank among the greatest philosophers of all time.

Plato is the earliest Western philosopher from whose output complete works have been preserved. At least twenty-five of his dialogues are extant, ranging from fewer than twenty to more than three hundred pages in length. For their combination of dramatic realism, poetic beauty, intellectual vitality, and emotional power they are unique in Western literature.

ROBIN WATERFIELD has been a university lecturer (at Newcastle upon Tyne and St Andrews), and an editor and publisher. Currently, however, he is a self-employed writer, whose books range from philosophy to children's fiction. He has previously translated, for Oxford World's Classics, Plato's *Republic*, *Symposium*, and *Gorgias*, Aristotle's *Physics*, Herodotus' *Histories*, Plutarch's *Greek Lives* and *Roman Lives*, Euripides' *Orestes and Other Plays*, and *The First Philosophers: The Presocratics and the Sophists*.

OXFORD WORLD'S CLASSICS

*For over 100 years Oxford World's Classics have brought
readers closer to the world's great literature. Now with over 700
titles—from the 4,000-year-old myths of Mesopotamia to the
twentieth century's greatest novels—the series makes available
lesser-known as well as celebrated writing.*

*The pocket-sized hardbacks of the early years contained
introductions by Virginia Woolf, T. S. Eliot, Graham Greene,
and other literary figures which enriched the experience of reading.
Today the series is recognized for its fine scholarship and
reliability in texts that span world literature, drama and poetry,
religion, philosophy and politics. Each edition includes perceptive
commentary and essential background information to meet the
changing needs of readers.*

OXFORD WORLD'S CLASSICS

PLATO

Phaedrus

Translated with an Introduction and Notes by
ROBIN WATERFIELD

OXFORD
UNIVERSITY PRESS

OXFORD
UNIVERSITY PRESS

Great Clarendon Street, Oxford OX2 6DP

Oxford University Press is a department of the University of Oxford.
It furthers the University's objective of excellence in research, scholarship,
and education by publishing worldwide in

Oxford New York

Auckland Bangkok Buenos Aires Cape Town Chennai
Dar es Salaam Delhi Hong Kong Istanbul Karachi Kolkata
Kuala Lumpur Madrid Melbourne Mexico City Mumbai Nairobi
São Paulo Shanghai Singapore Taipei Tokyo Toronto

with an associated company in Berlin

Oxford is a registered trade mark of Oxford University Press
in the UK and in certain other countries

Published in the United States
by Oxford University Press Inc., New York

© Robin Waterfield 2002

The moral rights of the author have been asserted
Database right Oxford University Press (maker)

First published as an Oxford World's Classics paperback 2002
Reissued 2009

All rights reserved. No part of this publication may be reproduced,
stored in a retrieval system, or transmitted, in any form or by any means,
without the prior permission in writing of Oxford University Press,
or as expressly permitted by law, or under terms agreed with the appropriate
reprographics rights organizations. Enquiries concerning reproduction
outside the scope of the above should be sent to the Rights Department,
Oxford University Press, at the address above

You must not circulate this book in any other binding or cover
and you must impose this same condition on any acquirer

British Library Cataloguing in Publication Data

Data available

Library of Congress Cataloging in Publication Data

Data available

ISBN 978-0-19-955402-7

16

Typeset in Ehrhardt
by RefineCatch Limited, Bungay, Suffolk
Printed in Great Britain by
Clays Ltd, Elcograf S.p.A.

For Kathy: aim at the heart

CONTENTS

INTRODUCTION

Phaedrus is named, as are most of Plato's dialogues, after one of the characters appearing in the work. In fact, *Phaedrus* purports to be the record of a conversation between only two people: Phaedrus, an upper-class Athenian and devotee of the new rhetorical learning which was popular in Athens at the time, and Socrates, who in the real world had been Plato's teacher, and in the fictional world of the dialogues is commonly Plato's main spokesman. The two bump into each other as Phaedrus is about to take a walk in the countryside outside Athens, to gain enough peace and quiet to memorize a speech he has just heard by the soon-to-be-famous speech-writer Lysias. The conversation that takes place between Phaedrus and Socrates is both interrupted and motivated by the declamation of three speeches—the one by Lysias (unless it is a Platonic fiction), and then two extemporized by Socrates himself in response. The topic of Lysias' speech was the relationship between a lover and his beloved in a homoerotic relationship, and so this is the topic of Socrates' two speeches as well. Lysias had argued that a lover is to be avoided in favour of a non-lover, and in Socrates' first speech he seeks merely to improve upon this thesis of Lysias, but in the second he entirely repudiates the content of the first, for its disparagement of love, and he calls this second speech a recantation, or palinode. After these three speeches, the conversation turns to the value of rhetoric in general, and what could be done to make it a true branch of expertise or knowledge, rather than something based on and pandering to more fleeting opinions. The contrast between knowledge and opinion is a basic feature of Plato's thought, and he always assumed that a philosophical life and worthwhile pursuits were grounded on knowledge and truth, rather than on more superficial values.

The dialogue is astonishingly rich, not just in terms of the quality of the writing and thought it contains, but also because of the number of allusions Plato has inserted to some of his most famous and central doctrines. Above all, we meet passing mentions of the theory (found especially in *Phaedo* and *Republic*) that there are transcendentally existing stable entities, usually called 'Forms' in English, which provide reference points for the identification of properties here on earth and thereby impart their properties to the changeable things of this world; of the idea (found especially in *Meno* and *Phaedo*) that all learning is recollection of knowledge absorbed by the immortal soul sometime before this incarnation; and of the doctrine (from *Republic* and *Timaeus*) that the soul or mind has three main parts, which may conflict. Faced with these allusions, some scholars of the early nineteenth century believed that *Phaedrus* was the first of Plato's dialogues, and that he wrote it as a kind of programme for the rest—a view that is now held to be eccentric. Many of the allusions, however, are so slight that it has been easiest to cover them in the Explanatory Notes (pp. 76–105). Here, in the Introduction, I propose to cover what remains largely by discussing the knotty question of the unity of the dialogue—a question which has proved of perennial interest to its readers. Does the dialogue have a unified structure and a single purpose?

Doubts about the dialogue's unity arise for one obvious reason: after the opening scene-setting pages, the conversation meanders from the first two speeches against love, to a volte-face, after which Socrates delivers his second speech, the palinode, contradicting the first and containing a complex myth about souls and their wings, reincarnation, and the power of love. This is followed by a sudden return to the topic of rhetoric, to see what measures might need to be taken to improve it: Lysias' speech is criticized, there is a discussion of rhetorical figures and techniques, a story set in ancient Egypt to illustrate the deficiencies of writing, and a final allusion to Plato's contemporary and rival educator Isocrates. Faced with this welter of topics, the nineteenth-century philosopher and social reformer John Stuart Mill, in his introduction to the dialogue, politely called it 'one of the most miscellaneous of all the longer dialogues of Plato'.[1] It is true that there are recurrent themes (above all, rhetoric, love, and psychology), but these alone are not enough to unify the dialogue in any meaningful sense. There is also a distinct change of register, with the first part (up to 257b, say) being far more poetic than the rest—far more mad, one might even say, compared to the sobriety of the last third of the dialogue. Despite all this, however, the dialogue itself claims that any spoken or written work should be an organic whole (264b–e), and one intuitively feels, partly as a result of the prevalence of Socrates' ironic tone, that there is an underlying unity to the dialogue.

At one level, one might judge the demand for unity misplaced. After all, *Phaedrus* purports to be a conversation between two friends, and it would be naïve to insist that such a conversation should follow a clear, linear path. However, the dialogue gives every impression of being carefully composed, and we do have the right to demand that a careful literary composition conforms to certain standards that a living conversation might ignore, especially when it is a philosophical work. In addition to the dialogue's 'formal' unity as a supposed record of a conversation between friends, we have a right to look for 'material' unity, a unity of subject-matter or philosophical point, an overriding theme to which other themes and topics are subordinated. In what follows, then, I shall survey all the major parts of the dialogue, before returning at the end to address more specifically the question of the dialogue's unity.

Erōs and Homoeroticism

All three of the speeches in the first part of the dialogue are about 'love', the word used in the translation as the English equivalent of the Greek *erōs*. Now, *erōs* is actually the Greek word for 'a longing capable of satisfaction',[2] especially passionate love, and in

---

[1] *Collected Works*, vol. 11, p. 62.
[2] Halperin [35].

the context of relations between human beings it means primarily 'sexual desire', or even 'lust'. Because *erōs* in this sense invariably has a sharply delineated object—it is not just a vacuous feeling of warmth or affection—it suits Plato's purposes, since his major enquiry is to ask what the true object of love is. Is it no more than it appears to be, or is it something deeper? In *Symposium* he answers that love is a universal force that energizes and motivates us in whatever we do, because its object is something we perceive as good for ourselves. Its *object*, self-evidently (at least, for Plato and his fellow Greeks), is beauty; but its ultimate, deepest *aim*, Plato says, is immortality—self-procreation in a beautiful environment. The highest manifestation of this is not the physical procreation of offspring, but the perpetuation of ideas in an educational environment in which the lover takes on the education of the beloved. This is the position taken for granted in *Phaedrus*.

Plato chose the term *erōs* from the range of possibilities because of its frankly passionate connotations: there is nothing insipid about a primal driving force. In *Phaedrus* he gives an astonishing analysis of what, in his view, is really happening beneath the surface of a love-affair, and focuses particularly on its ecstatic aspects—the ability of love to get us to transcend our normal bounds. Notice, then, how far removed this conception of love is from what we generally understand by the phrase 'platonic love', which is defined by my dictionary as 'love between soul and soul, without sensual desire'. On the contrary, 'sensual desire' has to be present, because it is the energizing force. It is also important for the modern reader to shed preconceptions about love which are based on Romantic or Christian ideals; in particular, Plato's constant association of love and desire (in *Phaedrus*, see 237d) may sit awkwardly with such preconceptions. As Plato makes plain elsewhere, when he says that someone desires something, he means that he lacks something (*Lysis* 221d–e, *Symposium* 199e–200a). We are not used to thinking of love as a kind of lack. Typically, Plato is talking about an experience which is superficially familiar to us, but which has hidden depths; he was always convinced that there was more to human beings than meets the eye, and it was part of his job to try to get people to see deeper inside themselves. So when he says that love is lack, we also need to see what it is that a lover's soul lacks, and it turns out to be the perfection of itself as a human soul—knowledge or self-knowledge. Someone in love has an inkling of his own imperfection, and is impelled to try to remedy the defect. This is not at all a base or easily dismissible conception of love.

Although there is little or nothing in Plato's conception of love which rules out heterosexual love, he invariably talks, as in *Phaedrus*, about the perils and benefits of homoerotic love. I use the less familiar term 'homoeroticism' because few Athenians were homosexual in the modern sense of being inclined to love *only* members of their own sex, and because it preserves the Greek root word. This emphasis on homoerotic love needs to be seen against the background of Athenian culture of Socrates' and Plato's time. In ancient Athens homoeroticism was considered perfectly natural. Usually, the same people were attracted towards members of both sexes, and in Athenian society homoeroticism was not regarded as perverted against a standard of heterosexuality as 'normal'. It was simply accepted that at a certain time of his youth a young man had a kind of beauty, and that older men would be attracted towards him. If an affair took place, it would be monogamous (there was little homosexual promiscuity in Athens) and would probably last only a few years at the most, as long as the boy kept his youthful 'bloom', as the Greeks called it.

Athenian homoeroticism was largely an upper-class phenomenon, as far as we can tell. There were two main reasons for this. First, any society which represses its women as much as ancient Athens did runs the risk of forcing its members to find other outlets for their sexuality. Respectable Athenian women would rarely even be seen on the street; their job was to keep house and bring up the children. This impedes the normal interplay between men and women which underpins a heterosexual society. Homoeroticism was more a feature of upper-class Athens, then, simply because these people lived in larger houses, with more opportunity to segregate their womenfolk. Then again, marriage was rarely for love. And another social factor was the constant risk of unwanted births: men practised anal intercourse, and intercourse between the thighs, with women as well as with their boyfriends.

The second factor concerns the somewhat ritualized expectations of a homoerotic affair. While a boy was in bloom (around the age of 13 or 14, say), several older men, in their twenties or thirties, would pursue him. They were the ones feeling passion, while the boy would most likely feel little or nothing beyond sexual arousal (Plato's scenario at 255b–256a of our dialogue is deliberately unusual). The boy was expected to be merely passive, to let the successful suitor have his way—to 'gratify' the lover, as the Greeks tended rather delicately to put it. This inequality is reflected in the relevant Greek terms: 'lover' translates *erastēs*, literally 'a man feeling *erōs*', while the boy is the *erōmenos*, just the object of the lover's *erōs*. What the boy got out of the affair—and this is why it was an upper-class phenomenon—was a form of patronage. In return for granting his sexual favours, he would expect the older man to act as an extra guardian in public life, to introduce him into the best social circles, and later, perhaps many years after the sexual side of the affair was over, to help him gain a foothold in the political life of the city, in which all upper-class Athenian men were naturally involved. Moreover, the older man was expected to cultivate the boy's mind—to be an intellectual companion. It was, in effect, a form of education. Greek education was pitiful: restricted to upper-class boys, it was in the hands of slaves, and taught no more than the three Rs, sport, Homer and the lyric poets, and the ability to play a musical instrument. In a peculiar way, the Athenian institution of homoerotic affairs filled a gap by providing a boy with a more realistic grasp of local culture and worldly wisdom.

Such homoerotic relationships were widely tolerated, but not universally approved (in *Phaedrus*, see 234b, 231e, and 255a). It was felt that there was something demeaning about them, especially for the boy, and fathers wanted to be sure that if a boy did enter into such an affair, it was with someone who would do him as much good, in terms of social advancement, as could be expected. This might seem calculating, but that is an aspect of Greek views on friendship in general: they frankly acknowledged that a friend was not just someone for whom you felt affection, but someone who could help you out. By and large, then, although there was no stigma to being either the older or younger partner in a homoerotic relationship *per se*, people turned a convenient blind eye to the sexual side of the affair. Lust in any context was never approved of. At any rate, we can be sure that Plato himself (and probably the historical Socrates) disapproved of giving in to sexual passion. The first evidence for this comes from *Phaedrus* itself, at 250e–251a and 253c–256e, but other Platonic passages are relevant: at *Republic* 402e–403b and *Laws* 636a ff. and 836c–841e stern injunctions are issued against giving in to lustful temptation. Plato's reasons for condemning the sexual side of homoeroticism are mixed. On the one hand, he thinks that giving in to lust of any kind is feeding and strengthening the base side of one's nature; on the other hand, he seems to think that the natural purpose of sex is procreation (e.g. 250e), in which case he would presumably be prepared to condemn homoerotic sex as unnatural. He has Socrates illustrate such restraint at the end of *Symposium*, in the famous episode of Alcibiades' attempted seduction. Socrates was undoubtedly attracted to the boys and young men who were part of his circle. At *Charmides* 154b ff., and especially 155d, Plato has him openly admire young Charmides' charms. His 'affair' with Alcibiades was even something his friends used to tease him about (see *Protagoras* 309a). But it looks as though he never gave in to sexual temptation, and merely exploited the traditional educational possibilities of homoerotic affairs. He became the boys' mentor, not their sexual partner.

If Plato disapproved of the sexual side of homoeroticism, why did he still use it as the background to his two great works on love? There are two main reasons (leaving aside imponderable issues such as Plato's personal preferences). First, as already mentioned, Athenians rarely married for love: a wife was for bearing children, while slave-girls were used for extra sex. Love, then, was more likely to be met outside marriage—and it might be a younger man who aroused it. And this goes not just for love, but even for the shared interests that underpin love: the educational potential of a love-affair, always one of the main things that interested Plato, was unlikely to be fulfilled in one's marriage, since an Athenian male had few shared interests with his wife and would not expect her to be interested in education. Second, with women being seen more or less entirely as sex-objects, Plato clearly felt that it was all too easy to get caught by the physical side of a heterosexual relationship. However, since Athenian society did place a slight stigma on the sexual side of a homoerotic relationship, a lover might well hesitate before consummating the relationship in this way—and such hesitation, vividly portrayed in *Phaedrus* 253c ff., meant that there was at least the opportunity for the sexual energy to be channelled towards higher, spiritual or educational purposes.

The First Speech

The first speech (230e–234c) purports to be by Lysias. It is a shallow, badly constructed piece—a 'clever' piece of sophistry designed to establish the implausible thesis that a boy should gratify someone who is not feeling love rather than an *erastēs*. It was precisely the use of rhetoric for arguing this kind of implausible thesis that gave it a bad name in fifth-century Athens. Since rhetoric was commonly used in moral situations, people felt that it could be used to distort the truth and make the morally weaker argument defeat the stronger. However, this speech was not designed for use in a legal or political context, but as a display piece—and even then, not for public consumption, since it was delivered in a private house, presumably to a small, invited audience (227b). In any case, Plato clearly saw the speech's faults: he has Socrates compare its content unfavourably with the works of famous love poets at 235c, and criticize its lack of organization at 264a–e. Where the latter aspect is concerned, the jerkiness and lack of structure of the speech are self-evident.

The main point of the speech is that love and sanity are incompatible. A lover is irrational and gets away with behaviour that would be found intolerable under any other circumstances: he is bound to be indiscreet and hyper-sensitive, and generally to make a nuisance of himself. But any possible charms this interesting or even amusing thesis might have are obliterated by the cold, calculating tone in which it is delivered. The talk is all of self-interest and advantage, and while pretending to have the boy's self-interest at heart, the speaker is clearly aiming for the satisfaction of his own lust. The central paradox—or possibly inconsistency—of the piece is that the speaker claims not to be feeling *erōs* for the boy, and yet wants to have sex with him, which in Greek terms is to feel *erōs*. Since the non-lover by definition is feeling no passion, the speech acknowledges and even applauds the merely mechanical aspect of sex.

Lysias argues that love makes men fickle, that emotional involvement spoils things by making jealousy and so on part of the equation, that a lover exposes his beloved to scandal and shame, and (233a–b) that the educational aspects of an affair are better handled by a non-lover too. Lysias wants us to ask: if all the supposed benefits of love can be supplied by someone who is not in love, and is therefore not liable to all the faults of a lover, what possible advantage is there to love? Since, as I have already said, the boy was not expected to feel anything more than affection for a lover, it is plausible for Lysias to have the non-lover appeal to the boy's calculating, rational side, which would not be impaired by passion, but the speech fails to acknowledge that people—any of us, not just lovers—are prompted by anything other than selfish motives, and do more with our minds than work out how to achieve these selfish ends. In terms of moral psychology, it is true that the satisfaction of some desires does depend on control of other desires, and so, in general, that reason and desire must collaborate, but this is the sole insight in the speech.

This may seem a harsh or even pompous analysis of a speech which may, after all, be no more than a light-hearted conceit, but such an approach is justified in the context of the dialogue, because Plato himself uses the first two speeches as cues to some pretty serious reflection.

The Second Speech

Not surprisingly, since in this first speech of his (237b–241d) Socrates undertakes to improve on the form at least as much as the content of Lysias' speech (235a–236b), there is considerable overlap of theme. We meet again the boy's fear of disgrace and concern for public opinion, the jealousy of the lover and its consequences in terms of an almost pathological desire for domination and possession, the lover's retreat once his passion has died down, his concern only for the short-term pleasure of sexual satisfaction, and the likelihood that he will ignore the educational potential of the relationship. These are the 'essential points' to which Socrates refers at 234e and 236a, and he does little more on these topics than describe them at somewhat greater length than Lysias had. Where content is concerned, he adds only the disadvantages of the age difference between lover and beloved (240a–e). Ethically, however, Socrates appears to have more genuine concern for the good of the boy than Lysias did.

The main difference between the two speeches is formal: Socrates' speech is much better organized. He starts with an elaborate definition of love, based on a simple moral psychology, and bases all that follows on this definition and on consideration of whether love harms or benefits the beloved. He draws on a traditional threefold classification of goods into mind, body, and possessions, and proceeds to describe the ill effects that a lover's jealousy has on his beloved in all three respects. A couple of paragraphs develop the disadvantages of a lover in other respects, and then the whole lot is summarized at the end: a lover is 'untrustworthy, bad-tempered, jealous, unpleasant, and harmful not just to [the boy's] property and his physical condition, but even more so to his mental development' (241c).

There are improvements, then, over Lysias' speech, but before very long Socrates issues a blanket condemnation of the speech (242d–243a). Later in the dialogue, however, he commends the formal aspects of the speech: it was good that it made a proper start with a definition of love and was well structured (263d–264e). As far as content is concerned, the only respect in which the speech is praised is for censuring 'left-hand' love—that is, love which feeds the base, irrational parts of the soul (266a). This love is portrayed as a kind of compulsion (240d) and as predatory. Socrates' final words are: 'Lovers love a young man like yourself as wolves love lambs!' (241d).

Plato invites us, then, to approve the formal aspects of Socrates' speech (at least at the level of ordinary rhetoric), but to think twice about the content. And it is obviously true that by anyone's standards it offers a highly distorted view of love. The most important aspect of the content, highlighted by an interlude in the speech, is the definition of love. This somewhat convoluted definition is as follows (238b–c): 'When irrational desire rules one's reasoned impulse to do right and is carried towards pleasure in beauty, and when this irrational desire has also been powerfully reinforced in its attraction towards physical beauty by the desires that are related to it, and has gained the upper hand thanks to this power, it is . . . called love.' Just as in *Symposium*, love is closely associated with desire. It is not defined as a kind of desire, but as 'the state in which a certain species of desire prevails over reason'.[3]

Again, there are improvements here over Lysias' speech. Lysias had assumed that all human behaviour—or perhaps only a lover's behaviour—is motivated by selfish desire. Socrates says that there are two sources of behaviour, irrational desire and a rational impulse for the good. This is better psychology, because

[3] Price [38], 61.

people are more complex than Lysias assumed. But in his next speech Socrates will develop an even more complex psychology, dividing the soul into three parts. One might think that this casts doubt on the two-part psychology of his first speech, especially since the tripartite psychology of the third speech is essentially the same as that found in *Republic* and *Timaeus*, where the soul is divided into appetitive, spirited, and rational parts. However, even in *Republic* we can also find a more simplistic division of the mind into rational and irrational parts, with the two non-rational parts being lumped together, and this is essentially what we find in this first speech by Socrates. There are no good grounds, then, for casting doubt on its content just because it divides the soul into only two parts. However, there are grounds for thinking that the way the bipartition is framed is too simplistic: the straight-forward opposition of pleasure and the good, though reminiscent of early dialogues such as *Gorgias*, is undermined in the palinode, where we see that the impulse towards pleasure is an essential part of a person's motivation, and that if his rational part is in control, this impulse can be channelled towards the good.

Another way in which the definition improves, in terms of content, over Lysias' speech is that it mentions beauty (at least, as the object of desire). Lysias didn't mention beauty at all, but it is clear from the third speech (and from *Symposium*) that beauty is essential to Plato's thinking about love. However, beauty in the definition prompts excess and lust, and feeds the irrational part of the soul, and this is markedly different from the function of beauty in the next speech, the palinode. The palinode reveals that love is not, or not just, a state in which the irrational part of the mind prevails, and that beauty appeals just as much, though in a different way, to the rational part of the mind. In other words, even if the psychology of the second speech is sound enough, there is no doubt that Plato would reject this definition of love. It is partial, at best: it describes *erōs* as 'lust', but not at all as what we would dignify in English as 'love'.

These flaws of content are the main reason Socrates rejects the speech so vehemently at 242d–243a: love is not the same as lust.

In addition, Socrates has so far fallen in with Phaedrus' tendency to treat speeches as a form of entertainment, rather than as vehicles for material that could change one's life. But there may also be another reason for his rejection of the speech: the passion of the palinode, and the insistence that there are good types of madness, suggest that Socrates found his first speech too cool and calculating. In order to understand and appreciate love, passion too is needed. This passion is conveyed by the brilliant palinode that follows.

The Third Speech (the Palinode)

Judging by the apparent flaws of the second speech, we expect to find in the palinode a less one-sided view of love—a view in which love and reason can go hand in hand, in which love is not entirely selfish but can be associated with educational and moral values, and in which, at the same time, passion and desire find their proper place. This is exactly what we find, but in an extraordinary context. In order fully to praise love, Plato felt that he had to explain its place in the metaphysical life of a human being. The palinode is about the soul; everything is either about the soul or is introduced to explain what the soul is and does (or can do). To be more precise, it is supposed to 'produce a conception of the soul and the Whole within which it makes sense to be a philosopher'.[4] The overall movement of the central part of the palinode is that it begins with the soul's vision of the region beyond heaven and ends with an analysis of the human condition of love. The suggestion is that we won't understand human experience unless it is put into a much larger context, and that the experience of love is essential for a human being to fulfil his highest potential.

The structure of individual parts of the speech is somewhat complex, but the larger pattern is clear. First, it is acknowledged that not all madness is bad; even Greek tradition recognizes three

[4] Griswold [17], 151.

forms of divine madness which benefit humankind (244a–245a). Second, there is a section on love as a fourth kind of divine madness (245c–257b). This section is divided into two main parts: a concise argument supposed to prove the immortality of all souls (245c–246a), and then a poetic and inspiring myth portraying the soul's vision of reality, a theory of reincarnation, and the effects on such a soul of love, which is now to be understood, at least in part, as the soul's recollection of its vision of reality (246a–257a). Finally, there is a prayer to the god of Love and a conclusion (257a–b). The meat of the palinode, then, lies in the second section.

The bulk of this section is explicitly acknowledged (at 253c and 265c) to be a myth or 'story'. We need to ask, then, if this detracts at all from its truth-value. It is clear why it is a myth: Socrates is talking of things that, even on the myth's own terms, could not possibly be known or demonstrated by rational argument, so he needs some other way to express what he feels to be the case. There are plenty of other times in Plato's dialogues when he resorts to myth in this way, most famously in the eschatological myths which conclude *Phaedo*, *Gorgias*, and *Republic*. Philosophy for Plato did not occupy a single register: there are matters such as the nature and experiences of the soul which the philosopher must enquire into, but which are not subject to dialectic or logical analysis. A certain amount can be achieved by argument (as Plato begins his discussion of soul with a series of syllogisms designed to prove its immortality), but there is more to say—more to speculate about. Plato uses myth, then, to supplement rational argument: if there is something impenetrable by reason that he wants to discuss, or an aspect of the argument that needs illustrating, he resorts to myth. This is explicitly the purpose of the main myth of *Phaedrus* (see 246a). The weakness of myth is that it is necessarily dogmatic; we are being asked to take it or leave it, with no middle ground. And this is the case even when, as at 246a, we are told that the myth offers us an incomplete picture, one which falls short of the absolute truth (though we are encouraged to think that it does not fall very short: see the second note on 250c). A dialectical argument offers us both sides of the case, but a myth offers only one. In the context of the dialogues, where argument prevails, this is a kind of challenge: if there is another side of the case, we are being challenged to figure it out for ourselves, to come up with a better view if we can. In this sense, while myths may offer truths or partial truths, they are only temporary.

So Plato gives us the myth in *Phaedrus* as the best he can do, for the time being, on the subject of the soul's nature and cosmic experiences. The myth, in its turn, is divisible into two main parts. First (246a–250c), there is a description of the entire cycle of what can happen to a soul (which is now assumed to be immortal): we hear of the tripartite nature of souls and how it is essential to a soul, *qua* winged, to rise up to the rim of heaven and attempt to see the plain of truth which lies beyond. Note the assertion of 249b that as human beings we must have seen the truth beforehand, otherwise we would not be human in the first place. We are not gods—we are not the gods we follow up to the region beyond heaven—but we achieve an unsteady vision of the Forms there. It is such a turbulent struggle that our wings may become damaged, in which case we fall to earth (become incarnated). If or when this happens, it normally takes ten thousand years of repeated incarnations and post-life punishments and rewards to regain our wings, with only one exception: a philosophical lover can use his memory of Forms, triggered by the glimpse of Beauty in his beloved, to regrow his wings within three lifetimes, or three thousand years, provided he can restrain his lustful horse to a sufficient extent. The description of the plain of truth is meant to be enticing enough to explain the attraction felt by a philosopher (literally 'a lover of wisdom') for abstract truth: his vision of truth was complete enough to leave him with a lingering dissatisfaction here on earth.

The argument of 245c–246a that souls are self-moving (and hence immortal), while bodies are in themselves inert lumps of matter, in need of generation into life, is here rounded out, since the self-motion of souls is imagined as their possession not only of wings, but of two horses to pull the chariot of the body. The wings supply the soul with its 'upward' impulse towards metaphysical vision, while the horses stand for 'bodily' motion (which is really a form of psychic motion, since bodies by themselves do not move). In the myth the ceaseless, restless motion of the soul is portrayed in its traversal of the heavens, and its generation of everything else by the idea of 246b that it cares for everything inanimate.

A person's soul is his most important part, because it is the soul's job to care for the body. But a major part of the application of this caring function of the soul is left implicit. If faced with the phrase 'what is ever-moving', and the type of argument Plato presents at 245c–246a, an educated Greek would immediately think of the (alleged) eternal motion of the heavenly bodies (see the third note on 245c). He would see that Plato was arguing that the eternal motion of the heavens was due to the presence in the heavenly bodies of soul (see also *Timaeus* 34a–b, 36d–e, 38e, 40a–d, 41d–e, 42d; *Laws* 898 a–e). Thus the eternal motion of the heavenly bodies, and their regularity, and the orderliness of the whole universe, are being attributed to soul. This is, in the first instance, how soul cares for the universe. But there is more: in Plato's metaphysics, a thing gains qualities by participation in the Forms. A thing is large because it partakes of the Form, Largeness. As soon as a thing is generated, it has such qualities. The Forms themselves, however, are perfectly stable and motionless. Somehow, soul is responsible for the attachment of Form-qualities to particular things—this is just a complex way of saying that soul is responsible for the generation of things.

The psychology adumbrated by the image of the charioteer and the two horses is fully compatible with the tripartite psychology of *Republic* and *Timaeus*, and even clarifies an important ambiguity. In *Republic*, Plato divided the soul into (in ascending order) an appetitive or desiring part, a passionate or spirited part, and a rational part. Psychic harmony and the fulfilment of one's potential as a human being, half divine and half bestial, are achieved when the rational part controls the other two. In

Phaedrus, then, it is quite clear that the charioteer is the rational part, the white horse the spirited part (which in *Republic* too is generally assumed, thanks to its sense of shame, to be a natural ally of reason), and the black horse the appetitive part. What is not fully clear in *Republic* is whether Plato considers these parts to have entirely distinct functions, such that the reasoning part can only reason, while the desiring part only desires, and so on. It can certainly be argued from within the text of *Republic* that the reasoning part has some desires, and that the desiring part can do a limited amount of reasoning, but nothing makes this clearer than the vivid description of the lover's inner conflict at *Phaedrus* 253c–254e. We see that the bad horse can reason, even if its reasoning is confined to prudential thinking about how best to achieve its lustful goals; and it is equally clear, from the violence of the charioteer's reactions, if from nothing else, that the charioteer is liable to emotion and desires. Plato even underlines the overlap between their functions by describing the charioteer in terms which are bound to remind us of a horse (he 'rears back' at one point), and by having the horse's complaints sound like righteous indignation rather than unbridled lust. The difference between the two is that the bad horse's reasoning is limited to short-term goals (just as Lysias' non-lover was too), whereas the charioteer aims for and considers the overall goodness of a person's life as a whole. The first two speeches assumed that gratifying one of the two lower horses was enough for me, but the palinode says that what 'I' really want is satisfaction as a whole. Or rather, the charioteer is *taught* by his confrontation with the beloved to consider the overall goodness of the lover's life: as Plato tells the tale, the charioteer goes along with the bad horse's desires until he comes to see what the consequences would be. By learning what he should not do, he learns what he must do. For Plato's moral psychology, the point is critical: the earlier speeches implied or said that reason should be an instrument of desire; now we see that reason has its own desires, which should control the other desires, if a person is to live the good life which is so often the topic of Plato's middle-period work.

In various dialogues Plato sometimes speaks as if the soul were simple and sometimes, as here, as if it were composite. In fact, though, there is no real contradiction. The soul in its highest aspect is single in the sense that all its energies are directed in a single direction, towards understanding. So in *Phaedrus* even the souls of the gods are said to consist of a charioteer and two horses (246a, 246e, 247e), but there is no conflict between them. Like a laser, they are all pointing in the same direction. Human beings can attain to this state, but by virtue of having been born in a mortal body, the purity of soul has become contaminated by different desires, and so the tripartite image of *Phaedrus* and *Republic* is fully applicable to us. The best we can do is restrain our appetites and our wordly ambitions, and compel them to work in harmony with reason's desire for the good. Then we become, if not gods, at least god-like—which is to say that we become philosophers. And *Phaedrus* adds that if we can do this for three consecutive lifetimes, we will break free of association with the body, of the wheel of reincarnation, for ever. In other words, we will have restored god-like simplicity to the soul, and since anything composite is bound to be destroyed (*Phaedo* 78c), it is only when we have pure and simple souls that we can attain immortality. As long as we are bound to the wheel of reincarnation, our souls will remain complex. Plato needs this complexity to explain a central paradox in his philosophy: on the one hand, he believes that everyone innately desires the good; on the other hand, it is plain that most people fail to go about even trying to secure it. Plato would say that the latter people have been overcome by their base appetites—they have not learnt to control the dark horse within them.

To return to the course of the myth, we are told in the second part (250c–257c) about the development of a human love-affair. The nature of the love-affair depends entirely, we hear, on how removed the older man is from the world (how ascetic he is, in a sense—or, in the terms of *Phaedo*, how much he has practised for death by separating his soul from his body): if he is fully mired in his body, all he will want is sex with the beautiful boy who arouses his love, but if he is a philosopher the vision of worldly beauty will remind him of heavenly Beauty, and his soul will grow wings and aspire to return to the region beyond heaven where he first caught sight of true Beauty. But Plato stresses that the philosophic lover will not want this just for himself: being attracted to someone like himself—that is, to a potential philsopher—he wants to bring out this potential in his partner. The educational aspect of Athenian homoeroticism is here properly fulfilled, in contrast to the situation envisaged in the first two speeches. When Plato says at 255b 256a that the boy comes to love his lover, he is saying that the boy comes to see his beloved as beautiful, since it is beauty that we love in the first instance. But this is to say that the boy comes to see the reflection on this earth of Beauty, and so is brought to recall the world of Forms. His education as a philosopher is well on its way.

There follows (253c–257a) a description of how the beloved is captured. This covers once again the course of a love-affair, but this time from inside the skins, as it were, of the two people involved, rather than from a cosmic perspective. The kind of lover you are on earth depends, to a large extent, on how successful you have been in seeing reality during your pre-incarnate existence. 'It will be the task of heavenly love upon earth to reverse the decline into incarnation, to undo the catastrophe. This will involve a cognitive recovery that both reveals itself within, and is assisted by, a generous relationship to another.'[5] Not only does the philosophical lover educate his partner, but (252e–253a) he also educates himself: he ascends the ladder only by pulling someone else up on to the rung he has vacated. The soul as a whole has to be redeemed, but since the soul is complex, this involves the reasoning part gaining control over the part(s) that fill the soul with cognitive blindness. The starting-point is the perception of beauty on earth, and the consequent recollection of Beauty seen before. The beloved's face is, as it were, transparent—a window on to the Form. There is much about this

___

[5] Price [38], 74.

experience that is unclear, but it must be the reasoning part of the soul that sees through the window, despite the fact that the whole soul—the whole person—is affected. The effect on the black horse is to provoke lust, on the good horse to restrain itself (i.e. to feel shame). The black horse temporarily gains the advantage—taking advantage of what must be a confusing situation for the charioteer, who does not quite understand what is happening in this dual vision of beauty and Beauty. It is only when the soul/person draws near to the boy that the charioteer realizes what was going on: he had a vision of ideal Beauty, and sees that therefore the sexual response is inappropriate. It will also be the older man's task to get the boy to see this inappropriateness, because the boy is at first inclined to translate love as sex (256a).

Some commentators[6] find this austerity puzzling—a reversion to the asceticism of earlier dialogues. They want to read the palinode as a recantation of Plato's whole pre-*Phaedrus* ascetic and rationalistic approach to life and philosophy, arguing that in earlier dialogues Plato would never have classified philosophy as a type of madness, nor claimed that the non-intellectual elements of the soul were necessary sources of motivational energy and that the passions, and the actions inspired by them, are intrinsically valuable components of the best human life. But this view, however superficially attractive, cannot be right, for the simple reason that in dialogues subsequent to *Phaedrus* (whenever precisely one dates it relative to other works) Plato demands a similar austerity from his philosophers. In any case, the extent to which philosophy is a kind of madness is uncertain (see the first note on 245c): it certainly does not mean that the philosopher loses his self-control. On the contrary, the central paradox of the speech is that 'losing one's mind is a prerequisite to truly finding it',[7] and the intensity of the experience of philosophical love, as Plato sees it, is precisely the intensity of the simultaneous presence in the lover of restraint and passion. It is true that the irrational horses are sources of motivational energy, but they do not fully

---

[6] Especially Nussbaum [56].
[7] Nehamas [4], p. xx.

co-operate. The black horse wants only fulfilment of its appetites; it is always pulling us downwards, away from the rim of heaven and towards earth.

So Plato's 'recantation' on this score is severely curtailed. He still regards intellectual attainment as the true and proper end for the soul, just as he always did. Appetite needs only restraint; it is not a driving force for the good. Just as a powerful stream of water can cause damage unless it is channelled, so the black horse's energy is good only when channelled in the right direction by the charioteer. The best human life, the life of the philosopher, still requires reason to be firmly in control of the 'bodily' elements. The more the philosopher recalls true Beauty, the more he restrains base lust. Emotional and sensual responses are allowed in the philosophical life only because they will not overwhelm the philosopher—and even this is not a new ingredient of the good life for Plato, since he always maintained that the philosophical life was not devoid of pleasure (see especially *Republic* 576c–588a and *Philebus*). But Plato is not—or not quite—making the implausible claim that emotional and sensual experience is essential to the philosophical life, as if only lovers could be philosophers. For instance, the dialectician of 276a–e does not appear to have any kind of sexual relationship with his student follower, but he is still the ideal Platonic philosopher. Love can make philosophers of any of us, but philosophers do not have to be or have been in love. Love is important only because beauty is the most accessible Form here on earth (250c–d) and is the primary object of love.

Though couched in terms of his own metaphysics and psychology, Plato's description of passionate love will strike an immediate chord with any lover—except, perhaps, in one respect. Conditioned as we are by the traditions of Courtly Love and Romanticism, we expect a greater emphasis on the individual as the unique object of love. Indeed, one commentator[8] has complained that Plato more or less ignores the individuality of the

---

[8] Vlastos [41].

beloved. On this view, Plato's ideas about love are deficient in two respects: first, he does not regard the beloved as worthy of love for his own sake, but only as he possesses the quality of reflecting the Beauty of another world; second, since love is lack, or a desire for one's own completion (see pp. xii–xiii), its focus is selfish and not on the beloved. Love for another human being is a sign of human weakness, whereas if we were free from this weakness, we would love only Forms.

The idea that it would be 'idolatry' to love and admire anything other than Forms is an inference from the religious awe with which Forms are invested in *Phaedrus*. But the inference is illogical—otherwise a Christian would be precluded from loving another human being just in virtue of the fact that the primary object of Christian love is God. Even in Plato, the gods love both Forms and people. Loving another person is not a sign of weakness, unless the gods are weak. Moreover, although Plato repeatedly calls the things of this world, including people, images or likenesses of Forms (250a–b, 251a), this does not mean that they are less than fully real (according to our usual standards of reality): it is just that we are being asked to revise our standards of reality upwards in the case of Forms. To love a person, on Plato's terms, is not to love a mere shadow.

In *Phaedrus* Plato makes it perfectly clear that a boy is not just loved for the benefits he brings to the lover—as a stepping-stone on his path towards philosophy and increased recollection of Beauty—but is also encouraged to develop his own potential as a philosopher as well. It is true that this means that the boy may not be loved entirely for his present qualities (warts and all, as it were), since the philosophic lover is looking to the future; but this is still a clear case of Plato valuing interpersonal love. In any case, in so far as we might value something as a means, that does not rule out valuing it for its own sake as well (compare the logic of the argument at *Republic* 357a–358a). Besides, the beloved in *Phaedrus* is said to resemble Beauty itself to a striking degree (especially at 251a), so that he may well be loved for his own beauty and other qualities. However, it is true that Plato would find it hard to conceive of love between ugly people, or immoral people (see 255b): in this respect 'Platonic love is peculiarly evaluative'.[9]

The idea that there are these deficiencies in Plato's views about love also depends on some philosophically difficult assumptions. Plato's theory is said to be deficient because it demands that I love someone just for her qualities, not as a unique and autonomous individual. But what is a person apart from her qualities? Isn't it precisely her possession of just her set of qualities that makes her unique? And is it at all complimentary to her to say, 'I don't love you for your qualities'? It is also possible that Plato's views on what it is to be an autonomous individual differed radically from ours, in which case it is anachronistic to require Plato to conform to our standards. Plato did not view an individual as a unique psycho-physical unit, since he separated body and soul; and even a person's soul is not a unit, but tripartite, with the rational part being identified as a person's true self. On this view, then, there is not a lot about a person that is lovable, if one is to love her true self. Nor does he believe that a person's ideas about herself and how she should live her life are necessarily authoritative, since he believed that there are moral experts who have the right to tell us what to do. And in *Phaedrus*, at any rate, he appears not to entertain the idea that individuals are unique at all: he has a theory of twelve types, not of infinite individuals, and in any case, whichever of the twelve gods one follows, the educational goal—as laid down by Plato in his role as moral expert—is the same: philosophy (248c, 249c, 253c, 256a–b).

Rhetoric

Rhetoric is a recurrent topic in Plato's dialogues, particularly as contrasted with philosophy. It was a major part of Plato's project throughout his writing and teaching career to get people to see

[9] Price [38], 99.

philosophy as the only worthwhile form of education, and to this end he set about disproving the claims of possible rivals: dramatic and epic verse, sophistic education, and rhetoric. A dialogue earlier than *Phaedrus*, *Gorgias*, is devoted to rhetoric and to the contrast between the rival ways of life philosophy and rhetoric promote. In modern terms, it is not entirely misleading to substitute 'advertising' for 'rhetoric', to get some sense of Plato's indignation that anyone should take rhetoric to be a reliable guide to a fulfilling and meaningful kind of life.

In *Phaedrus*, the question of the value of rhetoric is raised immediately after the palinode (at 257c), and signals an abrupt change of direction for the dialogue. Plato proceeds to extend the province of the term until it encompasses pretty well all genres of written and spoken presentations, public or private (257e–258c, 261a, 261d–e): the broadest phrase is 'the way both gods and men use words' (259d), which implies poetry as well as prose (see *Gorgias* 502c for poetry as a kind of rhetoric; then note 277e and 278c, and the description of tragic drama in rhetorical terms at *Phaedrus* 268c–d). The question is raised as to what constitutes good and bad rhetoric, and Socrates suggests that knowledge of truth is the criterion: only if a speaker knows the truth does he speak well. This is too simplistic: it leaves open the obvious response that someone could know the truth and yet fail to convince anyone of it, because he lacked the rhetorical skill to be convincing (260d). In other words, even if rhetoric is concerned only with persuasion, it might still have a part to play. But mere persuasion without knowledge is denigrated: without a grasp of truth, rhetoric will remain 'an unsystematic knack' (260e). Now, this is a reference to *Gorgias*, where rhetoric was defined in just these terms (at 462b–465e). So it looks at first sight as though Plato is prepared to modify his earlier disparagement of rhetoric (though at *Gorgias* 503a he did hold open the possibility of a morally sound, philosophical kind of rhetoric): if rhetoric can gain a grasp of truth, or if it can prove that it already has a grasp of truth, it will be a proper branch of rational expertise, as opposed to an empirical knack, gained by trial and error. Or, to use a dichotomy raised in *Gorgias* (at 454c–455a) and implicit in *Phaedrus*, rhetoric could aim for proper education, not merely conviction.

In what follows, Plato comes close to conceding that a successful orator must already have a grasp of truth. Orators persuade an audience by getting them to believe that X is Y, where X and Y are disputable terms (rather than obvious objects such as tables and chairs) and closely similar. But in order to be able to do this, they themselves must know the truth about X and Y—and in order to avoid having it done to him, any member of the audience would similarly need to know the truth about X and Y (261a–262c). But this turns out to be no genuine concession, because it is all couched in hypothetical terms: *if* an orator could do this, he would be truly skilful. Plato is not saying that a successful orator necessarily has this knowledge already. He is challenging rhetoric: orators *should* have knowledge, especially since they are dealing with important matters such as right and wrong. If rhetoric can prove that it has a grasp of truth, it will be a true branch of expertise. But that is an awfully big 'if'.

'Grasp of truth' is glossed as 'philosophy' (261a), so that true and valuable rhetoric, if it exists, is just the same as philosophy. How this is so is spelled out from 261a:

Even if, as Tisias and other authoritative rhetoricians maintain, the orator only has to concern himself with what is a *plausible ground* for accepting the particular factual conclusion for which he is arguing, and not with whether it is actually true, that does not absolve him altogether from concern with the truth. There is also the more fundamental truth of what it *is* for something—an act, a person, a thing—to have the property which the desired conclusion attributes to it. Without a concern for that, Socrates holds, one cannot come to know what to put forward as a ground for believing the conclusion. Thus the very knowledge of the plausible thing to say—which is what the expert orator *claims* to have—itself presupposes knowing the sort of truth—truth about the natures of things like justice, goodness and the other disputable terms which the orator's speeches are always concerned with—that in fact philosophical methods and only philosophical methods are designed to bring to light.[10]

A grasp of truth means knowing all there is to know about something, and especially disputable properties, so that it can be distinguished from everything else, especially other disputable properties. Knowledge of truth enables one to distinguish between things which are similar, and manipulate the audience's perception of these similars, if that is what one wants to do. How one goes about doing this is outlined in the method of collection and division (265d–266b): one should subsume various instances or types of instances under a general class, and then divide them, 'according to their natural joints', from genus down to infima species. This is a way to gain a clear picture of something, and how it differs from other things: if a human being is defined as a featherless biped, he can now easily be distinguished from a feathered biped, a bird. Two later dialogues, *Sophist* and *Statesman*, display such divisions at length (some would say *ad nauseam*), but in *Phaedrus* only two are illustrated (see the first note on 266b). Phaedrus professes himself happy to call this skill 'dialectic' or philosophy, but is worried that there may be more to rhetoric, specifically, all the skills and techniques that have been developed and recommended in the handbooks (266d). Socrates, however, is plainly contemptuous of all this, and claims that it is no more than general background information (268a–269c). Lacking a grasp of truth, rhetoric is forced to rely on formulae for organization and all the other tricks of the trade contained in the manuals. Socrates continues to insist that a philosophical perspective is essential for true expertise at rhetoric (and everything else: 269e–270a). Since rhetoric is the art of leading souls, in order to be a true expert a rhetorician has to know all there is to know about souls—in other words, to be able to distinguish all the various divisions of soul and the various different kinds of speech, and to know which kind of speech is suited to which kind of soul (269e–271d)—and be able to spot the different kinds of

---

[10] Cooper [62], 82.

soul in practice before him in the Assembly or lawcourt or wherever.

Looking back over the course of the discussion of rhetoric, we can see that it has been characterized in four ways: first, it is concerned with opinion rather than truth; second, its purpose is persuasion; third, its subject-matter is justice and injustice (in the courts) and right and wrong (in the assembly); fourth, it employs a variety of stylistic and compositional techniques. Plato has focused on the first two, while the subject-matter serves to emphasize the importance of knowing the truth, and the techniques emphasize the superficiality of the way rhetoric currently goes about influencing souls.

Two related views of rhetoric are floated in this section of the dialogue: first, that all it requires in order to be persuasive is a knowledge of what the audience *thinks* about a topic; second, that all it requires to be persuasive is the ability to argue plausibly. Plato has already dismissed the first view: the orator may be able to be persuasive in this sense, but the more important the issues he is dealing with, the worse will be the results if he does not know the truth (260a–d). But he acknowledges that he has not got to grips with the persuasive power of rhetoric, and this is why he brings up plausible arguments, based on probability, at 272d–e. But probability gains plausibility because of its similarity to truth, and Plato argues that this means that the successful orator has to be able to tell which kinds of soul will be susceptible to which kinds of near-truth, so that the successful orator still needs a grasp of truth and the philosophical expertise given by collection and division. In short, if there is such a thing as true rhetoric, a valuable and valid branch of expertise, it is identical with philosophy: it requires knowledge and uses the same method (collection and division) to reach it.

The demands placed upon true rhetoric make it not just unlikely (as Phaedrus ironically says at 272b and 274a), but impossible—or possible only for an ideal Platonic philosopher. There are a number of compelling reasons for thinking that it was precisely Plato's purpose to make true rhetoric seem impossible.

There is the inherent difficulty of getting the method of collection and division right, but this is compounded by the peculiar position of the orator. He is assumed to be dealing above all with mass audiences, and yet he is required to tailor his speeches to different kinds of souls. Suppose there are, as Plato suggested in the myth, twelve different kinds of souls: then the orator has to deliver—simultaneously—twelve different kinds of speech, because there will be people of all types in a mass audience. This is not just difficult, but completely impossible. Then again, he will be talking on a wide variety of important topics, all of which Plato requires him to know the truth about. Above all, he is supposed to have knowledge of the nature of the human soul, in all its varieties, and we have already been told, at 246a, that this knowledge is beyond human capabilities. The only viable solution would be for the orator to practise rhetoric on a single individual —but then he would become a dialectician or a philosophical lover, not an orator, because he would be practising philosophy and leading the soul of a single person (as the dialectician does at 276a). 'If conventional rhetoric does not become philosophical it is not a *technē* and cannot achieve its ends systematically; but if it does become philosophical it no longer wishes to achieve them.'[11]

If this is right, Plato does not really give rhetoric a proper hearing, and has not changed his mind about it since *Gorgias*. He dismisses its 'lower' manifestations as morally unsound, and as both based on and pandering to ignorance, and assimilates its 'higher' form to his own preferred way of doing philosophy. He fails to recognize, as he always did, that rhetoric is an important tool of democracy. The idea that there are two sides to every question, mocked at 261c–d because for Plato the truth is single, is the foundation of rational debate and legal practice, and if the ancient rhetoricians taught others to speak convincingly, this should be seen in the context, above all, of the litigiousness of Athenian society, where the ability to defend oneself could attain paramount importance. It remains today a fundamental

---

[11] Heath [24], 158.

principle of humane law that everyone has the right to present his case in the best possible light. In short, rhetoric and a liberal and pluralistic society go hand in hand—but as *Republic* shows better than any other work, Plato was deeply hostile to pluralism. A sound community, on Platonic terms, is a unified community.

The criticism of rhetoric and praise of Platonic philosophy gains a personal twist in the final page of the dialogue, where Plato subtly (see note on 278e) condemns Isocrates precisely for nailing his colours to the mast of rhetoric and failing to fulfil his potential as a philosopher. Since Isocrates was a rival educator, the theme of education, which has run below the surface of the dialogue, almost becomes visible. We see that on Plato's terms true education is impossible for a rhetorician: despite the importance of the topics an orator is required to address, his values are too superficial, and these are the values he would impart to his pupils. True education is possible only for a Platonic philosopher, who takes a single pupil under his wing and guides him towards the truth. If Socratic dialectic exemplifies true love, because the relationship between philosopher and pupil is exactly the relationship between philosopher-lover and his chosen partner, then rhetoric is false love—just another case, as in Lysias' speech, of a non-lover trying to persuade his audience of a thesis with no truth in it.

Dialectic and the Weakness of Writing

In the course of criticizing rhetoric, Plato has given us a pretty good sense of the contrasting ideal. A true art of speaking must have a grasp of truth; it should focus on private conversation rather than speeches; it must find resemblances where resemblances are to be found—that is, have a method of classifying into genus and species; and it must proceed in a systematic and organized fashion. In other words, dialectic is the true art of speaking. But this emerges only gradually through the section, and is only finally realized after a strange passage where Plato appears to find fault with all writing and, by extension, speech-making.

He tells a story—patently made up for the purpose—of how the Egyptian god-king Thamous criticized Theuth's invention of writing on the grounds that it would atrophy people's memories and make them rely less on recollection of pre-incarnate knowledge of truth than on ordinary, everyday memory, which is triggered by writing and other prompts from outside oneself (275a). The trouble with writing is that it cannot answer back: however many times you open a book, it still says the same thing, and you can't ask it to develop any ideas (275d–e). It is important to note that, despite appearances, this is not a blanket condemnation of the written word as opposed to the spoken word. The strictures that Plato places upon valuable use of words in 276a ff.—that it should be able to respond and that it should take place in private, in one-to-one educational situations—rule most speech out as well. Certainly, rhetoric as normally understood is ruled out: an orator delivering a set speech in court or before the Assembly is just as incapable of fulfilling these criteria as a book. Not all speech has a positive effect: speeches whose sole aim is persuasion are detrimental to the soul; only philosophic dialogue is truly educational. Dead speeches, like that of Lysias, can be persuasive, but you don't need knowledge to produce persuasion (260d). In order to be persuaded, you have to switch off your critical faculty, and trust in the speech and the speaker. This is precisely the kind of trust that is condemned as shameful at 277d–e, and it has perhaps been hinted in the myth of the origin of cicadas at 259b–d that speech can put one to sleep as well as wake one up.

So the problem may not be with writing *per se*, but with a particular use of writing. In the context of the dialogue, Socrates may simply be warning Phaedrus, the inveterate speech-lover, not to put speeches on too high a pedestal. How sharp, then, is the paradox with which Plato is teasing us? On the face of it, something extremely puzzling is going on. Plato, a prolific writer, condemns writing—and does so in a written work! Moreover, the Thamous–Theuth story, which commands us not to take written material seriously, is itself written down. If we are not to take written material seriously, it follows that we are not to take the story seriously either. This looks like a pretty paradox, and many scholars have read the passage as self-referential, so that Plato is condemning his own writing along with everyone else's.

But the paradox need not be so sharp. Above all, why should we think that Plato means to include his own writing in the criticism? The point is that Plato writes *despite* this criticism. If we feel so inclined, we could take the criticism in some self-referential manner, but there is no more reason to adopt this interpretation than there is to think precisely the opposite: that he writes despite this criticism because he thinks he has, to some extent, answered it. Of course he would agree that the highest and most valuable form of use of words is living dialectic between philosophers, or between a philosopher and a would-be philosopher, but he may well think that his chosen form of writing—the dialogue form— lives more than others and so responds to at least some of Thamous' criticisms. This is not the occasion for a full consideration of all the advantages of the dialogue form, but Plato might well think that his kind of writing differed from the writing of treatises, say, because it is more elliptical and ironic, and therefore engages the reader in her own philosophical quest along the lines indicated by the conversations of the dialogue. In other words, unlike a treatise, a Platonic dialogue is less concerned with giving answers than in provoking questions. Note also that 278c divides kinds of writing into speech-writing, law-writing, and poetry. It is hard to see where Plato's dialogues fall into this (presumably exhaustive) classification. Therefore, he thinks they fall outside.

It is only fair to say, before going any further, that this kind of approach to the problem has met with vigorous responses:

It is psychologically understandable that . . . the modern devotees of the god Theuth with his faith in writing have sensed the need to reverse Plato's judgment by affirming that writing in puzzles and allusions will indeed have the desired effect of clarity and dependability of knowledge in the case of the discerning reader. However, we must assert, calmly and without any polemic, that we are here dealing with a methodologically inadmissible supplementation of the text's evidence, and indeed a supplementation which leads to the opposite of what Plato intended.[12]

However, for all the rhetorical force of statements such as this one, it is a matter of interpretation. It is odd, though, that at the beginning of the dialogue Socrates insists on having Lysias' speech read out to him verbatim, rather than relying on Phaedrus' paraphrase, which might well have given Socrates the chance to question him (228d–e). But having noticed this oddity, we then notice some parallels. Lysias' speech is said to be a 'potion' or 'charm' (230d), and Theuth's writing is also said to be a 'potion' (274e, 275a). Thamous, then, stands in for Socrates: Socrates might have spoken to Phaedrus as Thamous spoke to Theuth, telling him that the speech he had brought was worthless, because it did not allow them to question the author. Socrates implicitly ridicules Phaedrus for his naïve trust in the reliability of the written word. However, the written word can trigger the memory of one who knows (275c). Just so, the first two speeches galvanized Socrates into producing his palinode, which we may take as a speech by one who knows (see 250c with the second note; and remember that the palinode was delivered in honour of Memory). So although Socrates, we may say, would have preferred the opportunity to question Phaedrus about the speech, for the purposes of the dialogue he chooses the written speech, just as for the purposes of the dialogue he is allowed to make an insincere speech censuring love.

The movement of these last pages of the dialogue also confirms this interpretation of the Thamous–Theuth story. It is only *after* the criticism of writing that the dialectician is introduced as the only one to survive the criticism. The root of the word 'dialectic' is the Greek word for 'conversation' (so dialectic survives precisely because it is a conversation between two people). We still refer to Plato's works as 'dialogues' because, with very few exceptions, they are dramatized conversations between people. From

---

[12] Szlezák [72], 41.

this simple perspective too, then, we can argue that Plato may well have thought that his particular brand of writing could survive the withering criticisms of Thamous. Of course the possibility remains that Plato may well have thought that the most profound moments in the philosophical life arise due to living interaction between two people (see also the spurious *Letter VII*, 341a–344d); but there is no reason he should not think that his own dialogues overcame Thamous' objections better than any other form of writing. In Plato's *Apology* Socrates is presented as the wisest of men because he recognized his own lack of wisdom, whereas others thought that they were wise; so we may take *Phaedrus* and other Platonic dialogues to contain genuine wisdom because they recognize their own limitations. They may fall short of the supreme standard of living Socratic conversation, but they are satisfactory second bests. Likenesses have been a theme in the dialogue; above all, an incarnated soul can rely only on likenesses to remind him of the supra-heavenly entities he saw as a discarnate soul. So Plato might well think that his dialogues contain likenesses of the truth, genuine reminders of philosophical conversation of educational value.

Plato has not quite finished teasing us, however. He has Socrates deduce from Thamous' criticisms that writing is only a diversion or an amusement, not to be taken seriously (276b–277a, 277e–278a), but then he has Socrates immediately describe his own comments as a diversion (278b)! Again, we are forced to ask ourselves whether we are meant to take this or anything else Plato has written seriously. But that is precisely the point: it is a feature of Plato's writing that he does force us to ask such questions, and in doing so we are responding to his writing in a way that quite closely resembles living conversation. In fact, Plato quite often, throughout the dialogues, describes writing, including some of his own, as an amusement or diversion (in *Phaedrus* the powerful palinode is described at playful at 265c, and see e.g. *Republic* 536c, 545e, 602b; *Parmenides* 137b; *Philebus* 28c, 30e; *Timaeus* 59c–d; *Theaetetus* 161e; *Statesman* 268d; *Laws* 688b–c); and then there are passages such as *Gorgias* 523a where we are invited to take his myths seriously, despite their fantastic qualities. This playfulness and teasing is designed, I think, to irritate us so much that we look for ourselves into the issues Plato is raising. Again, we find that Plato might well have thought that his own kind of writing avoided Thamous' strictures.

The mention of Plato's myths triggers a further thought. Another way in which Plato might have thought that he had responded to his own criticism of language is in incorporating myths into his work, alongside argumentation. At a simple level, it is obvious that myths survive through being constantly re-interpreted according to the needs of the moment or generation; even if this were not obvious, we are told as much in *Phaedrus*, at 229c–230a. That is, close to the start of a dialogue which contains a number of myths, we are told that myths need interpreting. Therefore, in including myths, Plato is engaging the interpretive or critical faculty of his readers, and not just letting the written word stand frozen.

At a more subtle level, there was a long-standing tradition in Greece for philosophers to write or appropriate myths, and these philosophers invariably used them to point up the limitations of the language at their disposal, and to allow themselves an alternative, non-analytic means of expression. Myths, then, allow Plato to write books that 'defend themselves' (275e, 276a, 276c, 277a, 278c) because they set up a dynamic within his dialogues which acts as a kind of dialectical prod to the reader, forcing him or her to reconcile the different 'truths' which they present (see also p. xxiii). This dialectic is, of course, not identical to the interchange between two living people, which Plato holds up as the only truly valid form of language, but it is an imitation of it, and as such—as a foreshadowing of the truly educational dynamic of living dialectic—it is supposed to spur the reader towards finding his own living teacher.

The Unity of the Dialogue

It is time to take stock and see what unity there is to the dialogue. There can be little doubt that Plato himself regarded the dialogue as unified, since he himself draws our attention to the two apparently disparate parts of the dialogue. The elaborate scene-setting of the beginning is paralleled by the scene-setting of the interlude between the two parts: there is a second reference to the cicadas of 230c at 258e ff., and there are also second mentions of the Ilissus, the heat of the day, and Socrates' and Phaedrus' comfort. He would hardly do this if he did not think there was some connection between the two parts.

Further echoes between the two parts confirm that we are on the right track. Readers will pick their own, but here are a few of the more important ones: the 'circuitous route' we are told at 274a that orators have to take to perfect their art reminds us of the 'revolution' of the discarnate soul on the rim of heaven at 247c ff.; the theme of gratifying the gods in 273e reminds us of the first two speeches, where the word constantly recurred in the context of the younger partner in a homoerotic relationship 'gratifying' the older man; rhetoric as 'leading the soul' (261a, 271c) resonates with the theme of leadership not only in the myth of Socrates's great speech, but in the playful exchanges between Socrates and Phaedrus at the beginning of the dialogue; the references to memory and recollection in 274e ff. jog our own memories to recall the doctrine of recollection of 249d ff.; the method of division and collection described at 265d–266b has already been concisely outlined at 249b–c (where, in fact, it is said to be an essentially human use of the mind); the half-truths glimpsed by the unfortunate listeners to an orator's manipulations (e.g. 273d) remind us that all these listeners, *qua* human, have dim memories of the truths they once perceived as discarnate souls (249b); finally, the relationship between dialectician and disciple adumbrated especially at 276e–277a inevitably reminds us, above all by the quasi-sexual metaphor of sowing seeds, of the relationship between lover and beloved in the first part of the dialogue. These are the sorts of echoes which are half glimpsed as one reads a work, and which leave one with the satisfying sense of something going on beneath the surface, some deeper level of authorial intent. In this instance, the intent is certainly to link the two apparently disparate parts of the dialogue.

There are two main overt topics in the dialogue—rhetoric and love—but only the first of these could make sense as a unifying theme, because there is evidently little about love in the second half of the dialogue. Some commentators, then, taking the dialogue to be a rhetorical exercise, say that the connection between the two parts is that the second part sets out as rules or precepts the faults or merits displayed by the speeches of the first part: first Plato displays two faulty speeches, and a good one, then he comments on them (including the comment that nothing is better than living dialectical conversation). There are more or less clever versions of this thesis. One commentator has astutely written: 'There are but three ways for language to affect us. It can move us toward what is good; it can move us toward what is evil; or it can, in hypothetical third place, fail to move us at all.'[13] He suggests that these three are exhibited respectively in the third, second, and first speeches.

All versions of this thesis fall at the same hurdle, however: they completely fail to do justice to the length of especially the third speech, Socrates' palinode. No reader of this speech can fail to think that this is more than a rhetorical exercise, that Plato is interested in the ideas presented there for their own sake, and that he is not just shoehorning them into what is essentially a dialogue about rhetoric because he had some new ideas on love that he wanted to air. Besides, there is actually very little in the last third of the dialogue by way of criticism, positive or negative, of the speeches of the first two-thirds. Moreover, since (at any rate on the view espoused in this Introduction) there is no such thing as true rhetoric for Plato, he would hardly be displaying it in the palinode or anywhere else. The palinode is not a piece of plausible

---

[13] Weaver [65], 60.

rhetoric tailored to suit Phaedrus' soul: it is heartfelt Platonic philosophy, designed to awaken Phaedrus' and anyone else's latent philosophical instincts.

The dialogue is evidently complex and Plato has gone to some lengths to preserve its complexity. A less straightforward solution than picking on rhetoric alone as the unifying theme is more likely to be successful, and other scholars have found various ways of attempting to do justice to the dialogue's many hues and layers. One might argue, for instance, that the first part builds up to a speech which displays rhetorical beauty, and then the second part shows how rhetorical beauty is just a reflection of philosophical Beauty, as normal rhetoric itself is no more than a pale reflection of philosophy. If one thinks that Plato is serious in setting up the possibility of true rhetoric, one might argue as follows:

In the second part we read that sound rhetoric must be conversant with truth and true method. The first part tells us what truth is, and how it is to be won; the second how it must be employed in rhetoric as an art of [leading souls by means of words]. If truth must be gained before it can be employed, if dialectic (whether under the name of [recollection] or not) must be exercised in gaining it before it can be exercised in employing or applying it, we need be at no loss to see how the second part of the *Phaedrus* grows out of the first, which is to it the necessary prolegomena as regards matter and method.[14]

On this view *erōs* is prominent because beauty has a special position: in the supra-heavenly world of Forms it shines with especial lustre, and here in this world it is the only one that can be seen clearly enough by the eyes to trigger recollection (250c–d). Hence, since recollection and dialectic are essential to the philosophical point of the dialogue, love and beauty are just as essential.

There are elements of truth in this view. Recollection in the first part of the dialogue does the same as collection and division in the second part; they are the same process, essential for the

---

[14] Beare [21], 318.

philosopher, under different names. Just as (in a process more clearly described in *Symposium*) the philosophical lover comes to subsume all his perceptions of beauty under the Form of Beauty, so a dialectical philosopher collects particular instances and subsumes them under a Form (I gloss here over considerable difficulties in reconciling the middle-period theory of Forms as assumed in *Symposium* and the theory found in the later dialogues where collection and division are prominent). Memory is an underlying thread of the dialogue, from the start (where Phaedrus wants to memorize Lysias' speech) to the end (where writing is criticized as destructive of memory). In the palinode, love and memory are critically connected: love is our reaction to the half-remembered Form of Beauty. The difficulty not only of gaining a vision of Beauty (and the other Forms) in the first place, but also of not being corrupted by forgetfulness (250a), is stressed. Socrates even ends his account of the region beyond the heavens with a brief prayer to Memory (250c). Then the lover and his beloved have to remember the god in whose train they belong in order to find each other and begin an affair (252e–253c). In short, love prompts recollection, recollection is the precondition for knowledge, and knowledge is the precondition for the right handling of words. In this way, all the major themes of the dialogue tie together.

There is a lot to be said for this approach. Its very looseness (compared to the search for a *single* unifying theme) allows it to accommodate the evident structural looseness of the dialogue, and it could easily be extended to account for the echoes listed not long ago (p. xliii). But it is a wide-meshed net, and it fails to capture one important dimension of the dialogue. If the themes of love and rhetoric are self-evident, there is also another, almost as obvious, which unifies them both. The dialogue is about the soul, because that is the place where love and rhetoric go to work. And it is therefore, in my view, about education—which is to say, about leading souls—because, as it turns out, both rhetoric and love (or philosophy) have an educational function.

In the first place, the whole setting is educational: Socrates wants to wean Phaedrus away from Lysias and towards a true conception of philosophy and love (257b). He is portrayed partly as a jealous lover, wanting to win Phaedrus' soul away from his beloved, Lysias, and partly as a lover concerned for Phaedrus' education. One might say that Socrates wants to win Phaedrus for philosophy, fails (Phaedrus shows not the slightest interest in either the content or the passion of the palinode), and resorts to showing, as a second attempt, that if Phaedrus' love, rhetoric, were to attain its highest manifestation, it would actually be philosophy. He adds, as a final appendix, that Phaedrus should not be fooled by people like Isocrates, who straddle the fence between philosophy and rhetoric. In this context one should notice all the play early in the dialogue with the phrase 'lead the way' and general talk of guiding (227c, 228c, 229a, 229b, 230c, 234d): the wrong kind of soul-leading is illustrated in the first two speeches, followed by the right kind, which is protreptic rhetoric, designed to encourage someone to take up philosophy. And notice that Phaedrus is the target of Socrates' weaning or guiding: 243e shows that he is the recipient of Socrates' words (coyly hidden behind the pretence that the recipient is a fictional boy), and 252b and 256e show that Phaedrus remains the object of Socrates' attention.

Rhetoric too is educational, for the obvious reason that moral issues are raised and debated by orators. As we have seen, Socrates broadens the scope of what is to count as 'rhetoric', until it includes everything that falls under a series of dichotomies: not just spoken words, but also written words; not just words spoken in public, but also those spoken in private; not just words in prose, but also in verse. Since lovers talk to each other, words spoken in prose in private may well be erotic in content, and so rhetoric and the art of love draw near each other. Rhetoric is meant to persuade, and a lover will try to persuade his beloved to gratify his desires (the Greek word for 'persuade' also means 'seduce'). The lover's search for the right kind of beloved to persuade (252e) is a specific case of the general principle that the true rhetorician must choose a suitable kind of soul with the help of dialectical insight (276e) and must search for the kind of speech proper to each soul (277c). If the true rhetorician is a dialectician, which is to say a philosopher, and a true philosopher is also a true lover, then the kind of intimate one-to-one conversation which lovers conduct is a good example of philosophical or true rhetorical discourse—not one that is written down, but conversation conducted in the heat of the moment, as teacher to pupil. Everybody has it in them to recall truth, and rhetoric and love, as educating forces, can help them to do it. So at 253b lovers are said to try to persuade their beloveds to follow a divine pattern—this is the highest educational aspect of love.

No Greek of Plato's day would be surprised to find this educational motif to the dialogue because, as mentioned earlier (p. xii), the educational aspect of a homoerotic relationship was taken for granted in Athens. Plato certainly stresses it in other dialogues as well: the whole context of several of the early Socratic dialogues such as *Charmides* is simultaneously erotic and educational, as Socrates uses his attraction and attractiveness to young boys to lead them towards philosophy; then several speakers in *Symposium* contribute to the topic (178c–d, 184c–d, 209c, and 210c). It is not surprising to find the same topic running through *Phaedrus* too: both the first two speeches claim, as we have seen, that a non-lover is better equipped to take care of the educational aspects of the affair than a lover; it is only the philosophical lover of the palinode who is capable of bringing out his beloved's potential; and the distinction of *Gorgias* (454c–455a) between education and mere conviction informs the discussion of rhetoric in the second half of the dialogue, as well as the description of the dialectician's relationship to his student, and even the mention of Isocrates at the very end of the dialogue.

So the dialogue is about love and rhetoric, as it seems to be, but they are connected because both are forms of soul-leading—both are educational. The first two speeches raise the question whether or not love is a good thing, and the rest of the dialogue answers the question in the affirmative. Love is good because it enables one to draw near to another person whose soul is of the same type as one's own, but is capable of becoming more perfectly so. This educational potential will be fulfilled provided the pair avoid the temptations of sex and channel their energies instead into mutual education (250e, 256a–b); this is the proper context of the praise lavished on the combination of philosophy and love for a boy at 249a. Speech is good provided it is one to one and the speaker gives the hearer's soul what it can accept and benefit from. Education, understood in the Platonic sense, is not putting information or attitudes into a soul, but (as the Latin root of the word still suggests) bringing out from a soul what it already knows—its pre-incarnate knowledge of Forms. This is what the Platonic lover and dialectician does.

NOTE ON THE TEXT

I have translated the Greek of J. Burnet's Oxford Classical Text (volume 2, 1901), except in the few places indicated in the text with an obelus, which refers an interested reader to the Textual Notes on p. 106.

The numbers and letters which appear in the margins throughout the translation are the standard means of precise reference to passages in Plato's works. They refer to the pages and sections of pages of the edition of Plato by Stephanus (Henri Estienne), published in Geneva in 1578.

SELECT BIBLIOGRAPHY

In this bibliography I list only works of general interest and relevance to *Phaedrus*. Some other works, which focus more on particular topics, themes or passages, are mentioned where appropriate in the Explanatory Notes (pp. 76–105).

Translations and Editions

All other philological commentaries pale into insignificance beside:

[1] G. J. de Vries, *A Commentary on the* Phaedrus *of Plato* (Amsterdam: Hakkert, 1969) (introduction, largely philological notes).

The best previous translations are:

[2] R. Hackforth, *Plato's* Phaedrus (Cambridge: Cambridge University Press, 1952) (translation, introduction, running commentary).

[3] C. J. Rowe, *Plato:* Phaedrus (Warminster: Aris & Phillips, 1986) (text, translation, introduction, and the best available philosophical commentary).

[4] A. Nehamas and P. Woodruff, *Plato:* Phaedrus (Indianapolis: Hackett, 1995) (translation, notes, introduction, appendix on Greek love poetry). This book is distinguished less for its translation than its excellent introduction, which has been separately published in A. Nehamas, *Virtues of Authenticity: Essays on Plato and Socrates* (Princeton: Princeton University Press, 1999), 329–58.

Nicholson [18] contains a translation of 241d–257b.

Plato in General

Plato is set in his general ancient philosophical context with admirable concision by:

[5] T. Irwin, *Classical Thought* (Oxford: Oxford University Press, 1989).

And there are two brilliant text-based readers:

[6] J. Annas, *Voices of Ancient Philosophy: An Introductory Reader* (Oxford: Oxford University Press, 2001).

[7] T. Irwin, *Classical Philosophy* (Oxford: Oxford University Press, 1999).

Among the many books on Plato, the following may be recommended for readers of this volume:

[8] P. Friedländer, *Plato: An Introduction*, 2nd edn (Princeton: Princeton University Press, 1969).

[9] G. M. A. Grube, *Plato's Thought* (London: Methuen, 1935).

[10] R. Kraut (ed.), *The Cambridge Companion to Plato* (Cambridge: Cambridge University Press, 1992).

[11] C. C. W. Taylor (ed.), *Routledge History of Philosophy*, vol. 1: *From the Beginning to Plato* (London: Routledge, 1997).

There are also two outstanding recent collections of essays, for readers wanting to take any issue or issues further:

[12] G. Fine (ed.), *Plato*, 2 vols (Oxford: Oxford University Press, 1999).

[13] N. D. Smith (ed.), *Plato: Critical Assessments*, 4 vols (London: Routledge, 1998).

Symposium

Symposium is very much a companion piece to *Phaedrus*, and readers of this volume will undoubtedly enjoy:

[14] R. A. H. Waterfield, *Plato: Symposium* (Oxford: Oxford University Press, 1994).

Books on Phaedrus

[15] R. Burger, *Plato's* Phaedrus: *A Defense of a Philosophic Art of Writing* (Birmingham: University of Alabama Press, 1980).

[16] G. R. F. Ferrari, *Listening to the Cicadas: A Study of Plato's* Phaedrus (Cambridge: Cambridge University Press, 1987). An earlier article of his ('The Struggle in the Soul: Plato, *Phaedrus* 253c7–255a1', *Ancient Philosophy*, 5 (1985), 1–10) is incorporated into this book.

[17] C. L. Griswold, *Self-knowledge in Plato's* Phaedrus (New Haven: Yale University Press, 1986).

[18] G. Nicholson, *Plato's* Phaedrus: *The Philosophy of Love* (West Lafayette, Ind.: Purdue University Press, 1999).

[19] L. Rossetti (ed.), *Understanding the* Phaedrus (Sankt Augustin: Academia Verlag, 1992).

Articles and Chapters on the Dialogue as a Whole

[20] E. Asmis, '*Psychagogia* in Plato's *Phaedrus*', *Illinois Classical Studies*, 11 (1986), 153–72.

[21] J. I. Beare, 'The *Phaedrus*: Its Structure; the *Eros* Theme: Notes', *Hermathena*, 39 (1913), 312–34.

[22] J. Cropsey, 'Plato's *Phaedrus* and Plato's Socrates', in id., *Political Philosophy and the Issues of Politics* (Chicago: University of Chicago Press, 1977), 231–51.

[23] W. K. C. Guthrie, *A History of Greek Philosophy*, vol. 4: *Plato, the Man and His Dialogues, Earlier Period* (Cambridge: Cambridge University Press, 1975), 396–433.

[24] M. Heath, 'The Unity of Plato's *Phaedrus*', *Oxford Studies in Ancient Philosophy*, 7 (1989), 151–73; followed by C. J. Rowe, 'The Unity of the *Phaedrus*: A Reply to Heath', ibid., 175–88; followed by M. Heath, 'The Unity of the *Phaedrus*: A Postscript', ibid., 189–91.

[25] W. C. Helmbold and W. B. Holther, 'The Unity of the *Phaedrus*', *University of California Publications in Classical Philology*, 14 (1950–2), 387–417.

[26] M. L. Morgan, 'Philosophical Madness and Political Rhetoric in the *Phaedrus*', ch. 6 of his *Platonic Piety: Philosophy and Ritual in Fourth-century Athens* (New Haven: Yale University Press, 1990).

[27] C. Osborne, '"No" Means "Yes": The Seduction of the Word in Plato's *Phaedrus*', *Proceedings of the Boston Area Colloquium in Ancient Philosophy*, 15 (1999), 263–81; followed by S. Levin, 'Commentary on Osborne', ibid., 282–92.

[28] P. Plass, 'The Unity of the *Phaedrus*', *Symbolae Osloenses*, 43 (1968), 7–38; repr. in K. V. Erickson (ed.), *Plato: True and Sophistic Rhetoric* (Amsterdam: Editions Rodopi, 1979), 193–221.

[29] C. J. Rowe, 'The Arguments and Structure of Plato's *Phaedrus*', *Proceedings of the Cambridge Philological Society*, 212 (1986), 106–25.

[30] H. L. Sinaiko, *Love, Knowledge, and Discourse in Plato: Dialogue and Dialectic in* Phaedrus, Republic, Parmenides (Chicago: University of Chicago Press, 1965), 22–118.

[31] J. Stannard, 'Socratic Eros and Platonic Dialectic', *Phronesis*, 4 (1959), 120–34.

[32] M. Warner, 'Rhetoric, Paideia and the *Phaedrus*', e-publication

from The Paideia Archive (http://www.bu.edu/wcp/Papers/
Lite/LiteWarn.htm).

Love

Love is discussed in both *Symposium* and *Phaedrus* in a homosexual
context. The essential book is:

[33] K. J. Dover, *Greek Homosexuality* (London: Duckworth,
1978).

As well as the introduction to [14], general works on love and related
topics in Plato's dialogues include:

[34] T. Gould, *Platonic Love* (London: Routledge & Kegan Paul,
1963).

[35] D. M. Halperin, 'Platonic Eros and What Men Call Love',
Ancient Philosophy, 5 (1985), 161–204; repr. in Smith [13], vol. 3,
pp. 66–120.

[36] C. H. Kahn, 'Plato's Theory of Desire', *Review of Metaphysics*, 44
(1987), 77–103.

[37] F. Leigh, 'Living as Loving: Plato on *Eros*', in D. Baltzly *et al.*
(eds), *Power and Pleasure, Virtues and Vices* (Auckland: Australasian
Society for Ancient Philosophy, 2001 = *Prudentia*, suppl. vol.),
96–113.

[38] A. W. Price, *Love and Friendship in Plato and Aristotle* (Oxford:
Oxford University Press, 1989). This contains by far the best
reading of Socrates' palinode, the great third speech on love.

[39] G. X. Santas, 'Plato on Love, Beauty and the Good', in D. J.
Depew (ed.), *The Greeks and the Good Life* (Indianapolis: Hackett,
1980), 33–68.

[40] G. X. Santas, *Plato and Freud: Two Theories of Love* (Oxford:
Basil Blackwell, 1988). His chapter on *Phaedrus* substantially
reproduces: id., 'Passionate Platonic Love in the *Phaedrus*', *Ancient
Philosophy*, 2 (1982), 105–14.

Recent debate about Plato's views on love was started by a typically
controversial paper by Gregory Vlastos, originally published in 1972:

[41] G. Vlastos, 'The Individual as an Object of Love in Plato', in id.,
Platonic Studies, 2nd edn (Princeton: Princeton University Press,
1981), 3–42; repr. in Fine [12], vol. 2, pp. 137–63.

Replies to Vlastos's paper include:

[42] C. Gill, 'Platonic Love and Individuality', in A. Loizou and H. Lesser (eds), *Polis and Politics* (Aldershot: Avebury, 1990), 69–88.

[43] L. A. Kosman, 'Platonic Love', in W. Werkmeister (ed.), *Facets of Plato's Philosophy* (Assen: Van Gorcum, 1976 = *Phronesis*, suppl. vol. 2), 53–69.

[44] A. W. Price, 'Loving Persons Platonically', *Phronesis*, 26 (1981), 25–34.

[45] F. C. White, 'Love and the Individual in Plato's *Phaedrus*', *Classical Quarterly*, 40 (1990), 396–406.

Psychology

Good general introductions to Plato's views on 'soul' or 'mind' are:

[46] W. K. C. Guthrie, 'Plato's Views on the Nature of the Soul', in G. Vlastos (ed.), *Plato: A Collection of Critical Essays*, vol. 2: *Ethics, Politics, and Philosophy of Art and Religion* (Garden City, NY: Doubleday, 1971), 230–43.

[47] S. Lovibond, 'Plato's Theory of Mind', in S. Everson (ed.), *Companions to Ancient Thought*, vol. 2: *Psychology* (Cambridge: Cambridge University Press, 1991), 35–55.

[48] T. M. Robinson, *Plato's Psychology* (Toronto: University of Toronto Press, 1970). His chapter on *Phaedrus* substantially reproduces an earlier paper of his: 'The Argument for Immortality in Plato's *Phaedrus*', in J. P. Anton and G. L. Kustas (eds), *Essays in Ancient Greek Philosophy* (Albany, NY: State University of New York Press, 1971), 345–53; repr. in Smith [13], vol. 3, pp. 18–26. And this paper in turn substantially reproduced an earlier paper: 'The Nature and Significance of the Argument for Immortality in the *Phaedrus*', *Apeiron*, 2.2 (1968), 12–18.

In *Phaedrus*, as elsewhere, we meet the doctrine of the tripartite soul. This has attracted a great deal of commentary, and the following is only a small selection:

[49] J. Cooper, 'Plato's Theory of Human Motivation', *History of Philosophy Quarterly*, 1 (1984), 3–21; repr. in id., *Reason and Emotion: Essays on Ancient Moral Psychology and Ethical Theory* (Princeton: Princeton University Press, 1999), 118–37.

[50] F. D. Miller, 'Plato on the Parts of the Soul', in J. M. van Ophuijsen (ed.), *Plato and Platonism* (Washington: Catholic University of America Press, 1999), 84–101; repr. in Smith [13], vol. 3, pp. 48–65.

[51] A. W. Price, *Mental Conflict* (London: Routledge, 1995).

Though she doesn't focus on *Phaedrus*, there is a brilliant account of Plato's thoughts on the passionate part of the soul in:

[52] A. Hobbs, *Plato and the Hero: Courage, Manliness and the Impersonal Good* (Cambridge: Cambridge University Press, 2000).

Three important recent papers focus on Plato's argument for the immortality of the soul at 245c–246a:

[53] R. Bett, 'Immortality and the Nature of the Soul in the *Phaedrus*', *Phronesis*, 31 (1986), 1–26; repr. in Fine [12], vol. 2, pp. 425–49.

[54] D. Blyth, 'The Ever-moving Soul in Plato's *Phaedrus*', *American Journal of Philology*, 118 (1997), 185–217.

[55] R. J. Hankinson, 'Implications of Immortality', *Proceedings of the Boston Area Colloquium in Ancient Philosophy*, 6 (1990), 1–27; followed by A. W. Price, 'Commentary on Hankinson', ibid., 28–32.

A controversial reinterpretation of the implications of the psychology of *Phaedrus* is:

[56] M. Nussbaum, ' "This Story Isn't True": Madness, Reason, and Recantation in the *Phaedrus*', ch. 7 of her *The Fragility of Goodness: Luck and Ethics in Greek Tragedy and Philosophy* (Cambridge: Cambridge University Press, 1986). This chapter substantially reproduces: id., ' "This Story Isn't True": Poetry, Goodness, and Understanding in Plato's *Phaedrus*', in J. Moravcsik and P. Temko (eds), *Plato on Beauty, Wisdom, and the Arts* (Totowa, NJ: Rowman & Allanheld, 1982), 79–124.

Nussbaum's reading of *Phaedrus* has met with a response from Gill [42], and especially from:

[57] C. J. Rowe, 'Philosophy, Love and Madness', in C. Gill (ed.), *The Person and the Human Mind: Issues in Ancient and Modern Philosophy* (Oxford: Oxford University Press, 1990), 227–46.

Myths in Plato

[58] M. M. McCabe, 'Myth, Allegory and Argument in Plato', in A. Barker and M. Warner (eds), *The Language of the Cave* (Edmonton: Academic Printing & Publishing, 1992; *Apeiron*, 25.4), 47–67.

[59] K. Morgan, *Myth and Philosophy from the Presocratics to Plato* (Cambridge: Cambridge University Press, 2000).

[60] P. Murray, 'What is a *Muthos* for Plato?', in R. Buxton (ed.), *From Myth to Reason? Studies in the Development of Greek Thought* (Oxford: Oxford University Press, 1999), 251–62.

Rhetoric and the Correct Use of Language

The best introduction to early Greek rhetoric remains:

[61] G. Kennedy, *The Art of Persuasion in Greece* (London: Routledge & Kegan Paul, 1963).

Plato's views on rhetoric in *Phaedrus* are usefully summarized, and their influence assessed, in:

[62] J. M. Cooper, 'Plato, Isocrates, and Cicero on the Independence of Oratory from Philosophy', *Proceedings of the Boston Area Colloquium in Ancient Philosophy*, 1 (1985), 77–96.

The relations between rhetoric and dialectic are discussed in:

[63] O. L. Brownstein, 'Plato's *Phaedrus*: Dialectic as the Genuine Art of Speaking', *Quarterly Journal of Speech*, 51 (1965), 392–8.
[64] A. W. Nightingale, *Genres in Dialogue: Plato and the Construct of Philosophy* (Cambridge: Cambridge University Press, 1995), ch. 4, 'Alien and Authentic Discourse'.
[65] R. M. Weaver, 'The *Phaedrus* and the Nature of Rhetoric', in id., *Language is Sermonic*, ed. R. L. Johannesen *et al.* (Baton Rouge, La.: Louisiana State University Press, 1970), 57–83.

Doubts about the Written Word

[66] R. Burger, 'Socratic Irony and the Platonic Art of Writing: The Self-condemnation of the Written Word in Plato's *Phaedrus*', *Southwestern Journal of Philosophy*, 9 (1978), 113–26.
[67] L. P. Gerson, 'Plato *Absconditus*', in G. A. Press (ed.), *Who Speaks for Plato? Studies in Platonic Anonymity* (Lanham, Md.: Rowman & Littlefield, 2000), 201–10.
[68] J. C. Klagge and N. D. Smith (eds), *Methods of Interpreting Plato and His Dialogues* (Oxford: Oxford University Press, 1992 = *Oxford Studies in Ancient Philosophy*, suppl. vol.). In the context of *Phaedrus* the essays in this volume by D. M. Halperin and M. Frede are particularly useful.
[69] M. M. Mackenzie, 'Paradox in Plato's *Phaedrus*', *Proceedings of the Cambridge Philological Society*, 208 (1982), 64–76.

[70] J. J. Mulhern, 'Socrates on Knowledge and Information (*Phaedrus* 274b6–277a5)', *Classica et Mediaevalia*, 30 (1969), 175–86.

[71] K. M. Sayre, 'Plato's Dialogues in the Light of the *Seventh Letter*', in C. L. Griswold (ed.), *Platonic Writings, Platonic Readings* (London: Routledge, 1988), 93–109.

[72] T. A. Szlezák, *Reading Plato* (London: Routledge, 1999).

[73] J. Zwicky, 'Plato's *Phaedrus*: Philosophy as Dialogue with the Dead', *Apeiron* 30 (1997), 19–48.

The Artistry of the Dialogue

Every writer on *Phaedrus* has to engage with the artistry of the dialogue, but some do more than others: Ferrari [16], Griswold [17], Osborne [27], and Morgan [59] are notable in this regard. Then see also:

[74] K. Dorter, 'Imagery and Philosophy in Plato's *Phaedrus*', *Journal of the History of Philosophy*, 9 (1971), 279–88.

[75] K. J. Dover, 'Poetic Rhythms in the Myth of the Soul', in L. Ayres (ed.), *The Passionate Intellect: Essays on the Transformation of Classical Traditions Presented to Professor I. G. Kidd* (New Brunswick, NJ: Transaction Publishers, 1995), 13–22.

[76] A. Lebeck, 'The Central Myth of Plato's *Phaedrus*', *Greek, Roman, and Byzantine Studies*, 13 (1972), 267–90.

[77] R. Rutherford, *The Art of Plato: Ten Essays in Platonic Interpretation* (London: Duckworth, 1995), ch. 9.

Phaedrus *and Post-structuralism*

The dialogue has attracted a certain amount of post-structuralist interest. The starting-point is:

[78] J. Derrida, 'Plato's Pharmacy', in id., *Dissemination* (Chicago: University of Chicago Press, 1981), 61–171.

Continuations of this line of investigation include:

[79] Z. Gregoriou, 'Reading *Phaedrus* Like a Girl: Misfires and Rhizomes in Reading Performances', *Philosophy of Education* 1996 (http://www.ed.uiuc/eps/pes-yearbook/96_docs/gregoriou.html).

[80] G. Whitlock, 'Concerning Zelia Gregoriou's "Reading *Phaedrus* Like a Girl"', *Philosophy of Education*, 1996 (http://www.ed.uiuc.edu/eps/pes-yearbook/96_docs/whitlock.html).

PHAEDRUS

SOCRATES: It's good to see you, Phaedrus. Where are you
going, and where have you come from?

PHAEDRUS: I've been with Lysias the son of Cephalus, Socrates, and now I'm going for a walk outside the city walls,*
because I was sitting down there for a long time, ever since
daybreak.* I follow the advice of your friend and mine, Acumenus, and walk along the roads. He says that walking there
is more refreshing than in the porticoes.*   b

SOCRATES: Yes, and he's right, my friend. But anyway, Lysias
is in town, apparently.*

PHAEDRUS: Yes, he's staying with Epicrates in the house near
the temple of Olympian Zeus* which used to belong to
Morychus.

SOCRATES: And how did you pass the time? I imagine that
Lysias was entertaining you all with a feast of words.*

PHAEDRUS: I'll tell you, if you've got the time free to listen
while you walk.

SOCRATES: What? Don't you think that I would count it a
matter 'above all time-consuming business', to quote
Pindar,* to hear how you and Lysias passed your time?

PHAEDRUS: Lead the way, then.   c

SOCRATES: Why don't you tell me about it?

PHAEDRUS: Actually, Socrates, you're the perfect person to
hear about it, because you should know that the speech with
which we passed our time was, I suppose you could say,
about love.* Lysias' work is designed for the attempted
seduction of a good-looking boy—but (and this is the
exquisite aspect of it) by someone who isn't in love with the
boy! He claims, you see, that you should gratify someone
who is not in love with you rather than someone who is.

SOCRATES: Excellent! If only he would write a speech about
how you should gratify a poor man rather than a rich one,

an elderly man rather than a young one, and so on for all the
d   other attributes which I and most of us have! Then his
speeches would really be sociable and would serve the common good. Anyway, I'm so keen to hear it that I'll keep up
with you even if you walk to Megara—up to the wall there
and back again, as Herodicus recommends.*

PHAEDRUS: My dear Socrates, what do you mean? Do you
think an amateur like me could remember and do justice to a
228a   composition it took Lysias, the cleverest speech-writer of
today, ages to write in his free time? Far from it—though I'd
rather that than a whole pile of gold.

SOCRATES: I tell you, Phaedrus, if I don't know Phaedrus, I'm
a stranger to myself too. But neither of these is the case. I'm
sure that once he had heard Lysias' speech he didn't hear it
just once. No, he nagged him to read it again and again—
and I'm sure that Lysias was very happy to comply. And I
b   doubt that even this was enough for Phaedrus. Eventually
he borrowed the scroll himself and pored over those parts of
the speech he particularly wanted to look at, and continued
with this, sitting in his place from daybreak onwards, until
he got tired and went for a walk, by which time, I would say
—yes, by the dog,* I would!—he knew the speech by heart,
unless it was really quite long. And so he went for a walk
outside the city walls to rehearse the speech. Then he came
across someone who is sick with passion for hearing
speeches.* When he saw him . . . well, when he saw him he
was delighted to find someone with whom he could share
his frenzy, so he told him to lead the way. But when this
c   speech-lover asked him to repeat the speech, he coyly
pretended that he didn't want to, even though he was eventually going to repeat it even if he had to force it on an
unwilling audience.* So, Phaedrus, why don't you ask him
right here and now to do what he's soon going to do
anyway?

PHAEDRUS: It's certainly true that I'll be far better off if
I repeat it as best I can, since I don't think you're ever

4

going to let me go until I've made some sort of attempt at reciting it.

SOCRATES: You're quite right.

PHAEDRUS: Here's what I'll do, then. You see, in actual fact, d Socrates, I honestly didn't learn it word for word. But I shall go through the general sense of almost all the points of difference, according to Lysias, between the behaviour of the lover and that of the non-lover, and summarize each point in order, from first to last.

SOCRATES: Yes, but first, my friend, show me what you've got in your left hand under your clothing. I suspect you've got the actual speech. If I'm right, you should know that, fond as I am of you, I have no intention of letting you practise on me when Lysias is here too. Come on, then, show me what e you've got.*

PHAEDRUS (*producing the written speech**): Enough! Socrates, you've dashed my hope of using you as my training-ground. But where would you like us to sit down and read the piece?

SOCRATES: Let's turn off the road here and walk alongside the 229a Ilissus.* Then we can find somewhere quiet to sit down, wherever we like.

PHAEDRUS: It turns out to be a good thing that I have no shoes on. You never do, of course.* It will be very easy for us to wet our feet as we walk by the stream, which will be nice, especially at this time of day in this season.

SOCRATES: Lead the way, then, and at the same time think about where we might sit.

PHAEDRUS: Do you see that very tall plane tree?

SOCRATES: Of course.

PHAEDRUS: It's shady and breezy there, and there's grass for b sitting on, or lying on if we like.

SOCRATES: Lead the way, please.

PHAEDRUS: Tell me, Socrates, isn't this or hereabouts the place from where Boreas is said to have abducted Oreithuia from the Ilissus?

SOCRATES: Yes, that's how the story goes, anyway.

5

PHAEDRUS: Well, wasn't it from here? At any rate, the water has a pleasant, clean, clear appearance—just right for girls to play beside.

c SOCRATES: No, this isn't the place. It's about two or three stades* downstream, where one crosses to go towards Agra.* There's an altar of Boreas somewhere there.

PHAEDRUS: I've not really noticed it. But tell me, Socrates, by Zeus:* do you think this story is true?

SOCRATES: It wouldn't be odd for me to doubt it as the experts do. I might give a clever explanation of it, and say that a gust of wind from the north pushed her from the nearby rocks while she was playing with Pharmaceia, and although this caused her death she was said to have been abducted by Boreas—either from here or from the Areopa-

d gus,* since there's another version of the story, that she was abducted from there, not here. Basically, Phaedrus, although I find these kinds of interpretations fascinating, they are the work of someone who is too clever for his own good. He has to work hard and is rather unfortunate, if only because he next has to correct the way Centaurs look, and then the Chimaera, and then there pours down on him a horde of similar creatures, like the Gorgon and Pegasus and count-

e less other extraordinary beasts with all kinds of monstrous natures.*† If anyone has doubts about these creatures and wants to use a rough-and-ready kind of ingenuity to force each of them to conform with probability, he'll need a lot of spare time. As for me, I never have time to spend on these things, and there's a good reason for this, my friend: I am still incapable of obeying the Delphic inscription and know-ing myself.* It strikes me as absurd to look into matters that have nothing to do with me as long as I'm still ignorant in

230a this respect, so I ignore all these matters and go along with the traditional views about them. As I said just now, I investigate myself rather than these things, to see whether I am in fact a creature of more complexity and savagery than Typhon, or something tamer and more simple, with a

naturally divine and non-Typhonic nature. But anyway, my
friend, if I may interrupt our conversation, isn't this the tree
you were taking us to?

PHAEDRUS: Yes, this is the one.   b

SOCRATES: By Hera, what a lovely secluded spot! This plane
tree is very tall and flourishing, the agnus is tall enough to
provide excellent shade too, and since it is in full bloom it
will probably make the place especially fragrant. Then
again, the stream flowing under the plane tree is particularly
charming, and its water is very cold, to judge by my foot.
The place seems by the statuettes and figures* to be sacred to
certain of the Nymphs and to Achelous. Or again, if you
like, how pleasant and utterly delightful is the freshness c
of the air here! The whisper of the breeze chimes in a
summery, clear way with the chorus of the cicadas. But
the nicest thing of all is the fact that the grass is on a
gentle slope which is perfect for resting one's head on when
lying down. You are indeed a very good guide, my dear
Phaedrus.

PHAEDRUS: You're quite remarkable, Socrates! You're like a
complete stranger—literally, as you say, as if you were a
visitor being shown around, not a local resident. It's proof
of how you never leave town either to travel abroad or even, d
I think, to step outside the city walls at all.

SOCRATES: You'll have to forgive me, my friend. I'm an intellectual, you see, and country places with their trees tend to
have nothing to teach me, whereas people in town do.* But I
think you've found a way to charm me outside. Just as
people get hungry animals to follow them by waving some
greenery or a vegetable in front of them, so it looks as
though all you have to do is dangle a speech on a scroll in
front of me and you can take me all over Attica, and any- e
where else you fancy. At the moment, though, this is the
place I've come to, and so I think I'll lie down, and you can
find whatever position you think will be most comfortable
for reading, and then read.

7

PHAEDRUS: Here I go, then.*

'You are aware of my situation and you have heard me explain how, in my opinion, it would be to our advantage if this were to happen.* I think that the fact that I happen not to be in love 231a with you should not prevent me getting what I want. You should know that a lover regrets the favours he does once his desire comes to an end, whereas it stands to reason that there is never a time when a non-lover will change his mind. For if he exerts himself to do a favour, he does so willingly, not because he is driven by an irresistible force, and as the best way he can think of to further his own interests.

'Moreover, a lover thinks about how he has harmed his own affairs as a result of being in love and about the favours he has done his beloved, takes into consideration all the effort he has put in as well, and concludes that he has long ago paid his
b beloved the equivalent of any favours he might receive. A non-lover, however, cannot make being in love an excuse for the neglect of his own business, or take past effort into account, or complain of having fallen out with his relatives. The upshot is that, lacking any of these difficulties, he is left with nothing except to commit himself to doing whatever he thinks will please the other party.

'Moreover, if a lover deserves to be valued because he claims
c to be so very fond of his beloved that he is ready to incur the hatred of everyone else both by what he says and by what he does in order to please his beloved, it is easy to see that, if this claim of his is true, he will value anyone with whom he subsequently falls in love more than his present beloved, and it goes without saying that he will treat him badly if that is what his new beloved wants him to do.

'Also, how does it make sense to give away such a precious thing* to someone suffering from the kind of affliction which
d stops those who experience it even trying to get rid of it? After all, a lover admits that he is sick rather than in his right mind; he knows he is deranged, but is incapable of self-control. And

8

so, when he returns to his senses, how could he think that the decisions he made when he was in this deranged state are sound?

'Then again, if you were to pick the best man from among your lovers, you would have a small field from which to make your choice. But if you were to pick a partner who was most suited to you from among everyone else, you would have a large field to choose from. And so the large field offers you a much better chance of finding someone worthy of your e affection.

'Now, if you are worried about the moral code—about the stigma that might attach to you if people found out—it stands to reason that a lover, because he thinks that everyone else 232a considers him just as happy as he does himself, will be stimulated by talking about it, and will proudly point out to everyone that his efforts were not in vain, while a non-lover, who is in control of himself, will choose the best course of action, rather than a worldly reputation.

'Moreover, a lover is bound to be found out. He will be seen by many people trailing along after his beloved and making this his chief business, and so when he and his beloved are spotted talking to each other, people think they are together at that time because they have just satisfied their desires or are b just about to. But it never even crosses their minds to criticize non-lovers for spending time together, because they realize that conversation is inevitable between friends or people enjoying themselves in some other way.

'Also, if you are worried by the thought that it is hard for a relationship to last, but that although breaking up normally troubles both friends equally, it would be you who would suffer badly since you have given away what you value most,* it is c reasonable for you to be more concerned about a lover than a non-lover, because a lover is easily upset and thinks that everything is designed to do him harm. That is also why he tries to stop his beloved spending time with others, because he is afraid that those who are well off will prove to have more

9

money than him and that those who have been educated will
be more knowledgeable than him—and he is concerned about
what anyone with any other advantage might be able to do. A
d lover will therefore persuade you to put these people off, until
you reach a state of complete isolation from friends, and if you
are more clever than him and look to your own advantage, you
will cause a rift between yourself and him. Someone who is not
in love, however, but got what he wanted as a result of his
excellent qualities, will not mind others spending time with
you, and in fact will be deeply suspicious of an unwillingness
to do so, which he will take as a sign of their wanting to have
nothing to do with him, while he will think of the benefit he
could gain from those who do spend time with you. The
upshot is that a non-lover can be far more hopeful of gaining
e friendship rather than antagonism as a result of the affair.

'Also, it is commonly the case that a lover desires his beloved's body before he has come to appreciate his character or got
to know his other attributes. This should make the beloved
wonder whether a lover will still want to be his friend when his
desire has come to an end. A couple who are not in love,
233a however, were friendly with each other even before they con-
summated their affair, and the favours they do each other are
unlikely to lessen their friendship, but are more likely to
remain as indicators of more to come in the future.

'Also, you can expect to become a better person if you listen
to what I say than if you listen to a lover. A lover praises the
things his beloved says and does even when they do not
conform with morality, partly because he is afraid of being
disliked, partly because his judgement is impaired by his
b desire. After all, here are some typical manifestations of love.
Love makes a lover count as disastrous setbacks which cause
no one else any distress at all, and when things are going well
love compels him to praise even things which ought not to give
him pleasure. Pity, then, rather than admiration, would be a
far more appropriate response for a beloved to show a lover.
But if you listen to me, first, when I am with you, I will not be

a slave to immediate pleasure, but will look to the beneficial
future results of our relationship; I will not be overcome by c
love, but will be in control of myself; I will not let trivia arouse
me to violent hostility, though important issues will gradually
make me a little angry; I will forgive unintentional errors and
try to stop you making intentional mistakes before they happen. This all goes to show that our relationship would last a
long time.

'If it happens to have occurred to you that there can be no
real warmth in a relationship unless your partner is in love,
you should bear in mind that, if this were so, we would not d
value our sons or parents, nor would we have good friends,
whose friendship does not depend on the kind of desire a lover
has, but on other aspirations.*

'Moreover, it follows from the principle that we should
make a particular point of gratifying those who particularly
need our favours, that in other respects too it is the most needy
people, rather than the best people, whom we should be helping, since they will be especially grateful for their release from
especially grim circumstances. And the same goes for our private dinner-parties too: we should not invite our friends, but e
those who beg for food and need filling up, because it is they
who will be appreciative, who will follow us around, call at our
house, feel the greatest pleasure, be extremely grateful, and
pray for us to be showered with blessings. No, perhaps you
should gratify those who are best able to repay the favour,
rather than those who are especially needy; those who deserve
what you have to give, rather than those who merely beg for it; 234a
those who will share their own goods with you when you are
older, rather than those who merely appreciate your youthful
charms; those who will always maintain a discreet silence,
rather than those who will boast to others of their success;
those who will be lifelong friends, rather than those who pursue you for a short while; those who will take the passing of
your youthful charms† as an opportunity to display their own
good qualities, rather than those who will make the end of

their desire an excuse for breaking up with you. You should
b remember what I have been saying and bear this in mind:
while in the case of lovers their friends tell them off for the
depravity of what they are up to, no friend or relation has ever
criticized a non-lover for letting an affair impair his judgement
about what is best for himself.

'Now, you might be wondering, perhaps, whether I am
suggesting that you gratify every man who is not in love with
you. In the first place, I am sure that a lover would not tell
you to have this attitude towards every lover either, because
c then the favours you grant would not deserve the same degree
of gratitude from their recipients, nor, if you wanted to,
would you be able to keep an affair secret from everyone else
as well as you might otherwise. In the second place, then, no
harm should accrue from this business, but only good, for
both parties.

'I think that I have said enough to make my point. If you
think I have left anything out and you want to hear further
arguments, you have only to ask.'

So how does the speech strike you, Socrates? Isn't it
extraordinary, especially in its use of language?
d SOCRATES: Yes, it's out of this world, my friend. I was
amazed. And you were the reason I felt this way, Phaedrus,
because I was looking at you while you were reading, and it
seemed to me that the speech made you glow with pleasure.
Assuming that your understanding of these matters is better
than mine, I followed your lead, and so I came to share the
ecstasy of your enthusiasm.*
PHAEDRUS: Hmm . . . does it strike you as something to joke
about like this?
SOCRATES: Do you think I'm joking? Do you think I'm
anything less than serious?
e PHAEDRUS: Not at all, Socrates. But please—I beg you in the
name of Zeus the guardian of friendship—give me your
honest opinion: do you think anyone else in Greece could

compose a more important speech on this topic, or could find anything to add to it?

SOCRATES: What? Are we also required to praise a speech because its writer has included the necessary content, and not just because he has written a clear and compact speech, and has finely honed his vocabulary? If we are, I'll have to take your word for it, because it went over my useless head. I was paying attention only to the form of the speech, and I 235a got the impression† that even Lysias himself was dissatisfied with the content. In fact, Phaedrus, unless you correct me, I thought he repeated himself two or three times, as if he had some difficulty finding a lot to say on the subject, or perhaps because he wasn't interested in such matters. And so I thought that in an immature fashion he was showing off his ability to say the same thing in two different ways and to find both times an excellent way of expressing himself.

PHAEDRUS: You're talking nonsense, Socrates. The best b aspect of the speech is exactly what passed you by. He has omitted none of the topics implicit within the subject-matter which are worth mentioning, and so no one could possibly address the matter more fully and more valuably than he has in what he has said.

SOCRATES: Now you've gone too far. I can't go along with you, because the skilful men and women of old who have spoken and written about these matters will challenge me if I agree with you just to please you.

PHAEDRUS: Who are you talking about? Where have you c heard a better treatment than this?

SOCRATES: I can't tell you right now, just like that. But I must have heard someone—perhaps the fair Sappho, or Anacreon the wise,* or even some prose-writer or other. What's my evidence for this? My breast is full, you might say, my friend, and I feel that I could add to what Lysias said on the subject, and do no worse than he did too. But awareness of my own ignorance makes me certain that I didn't gain any of these ideas from my own resources, and so the only

alternative, it seems to me, is that I have been filled, like a
d   jug, by streams flowing from elsewhere through my ears.
But I've actually forgotten—under the influence of my
stupidity again—how and from whom I heard them.

PHAEDRUS: An excellent speech, Socrates—and extremely
generous! I mean, don't let me insist that you tell me from
whom and how you heard them, but do exactly what you've
said. You undertook to make a new and better speech than
the one on the scroll, no shorter than his, and without
touching on his points. And I in my turn, in imitation of the
nine archons, undertake to dedicate a life-size golden statue
e   in Delphi not only of myself, but also of you.*

SOCRATES: You're very kind, Phaedrus, and truly golden, if
you think I'm claiming that Lysias has completely missed
the mark, and that I could add to all he has already said. I
doubt that even the worst writer would get everything completely wrong. For instance, to take the topic of the speech,
who do you think would fail to support the claim that one
should gratify a non-lover rather than a lover by praising
the common sense of the former and criticizing the
derangement of the latter? These points are essential to the
236a   argument: do you think anyone would say anything different? No, I think we should ignore points of this kind and
forgive the speaker for making them. Where points of this
kind are concerned, we should praise arrangement rather
than inventiveness. But we should praise inventiveness as
well as arrangement when the points are inessential and are
hard to invent.

PHAEDRUS: I agree with you. I think you've made a fair point.
And I'll do likewise as well: I'll grant your assumption that a
b   lover is more deranged than a non-lover, and if in what
remains you can add to what has already been said and
produce a more valuable speech, your likeness in beaten
metal will be erected next to the offering of the Cypselids in
Olympia.

SOCRATES: Phaedrus, are you cross at my criticism of your

beloved, which was only meant to tease you? Do you think that I would really try to surpass his cleverness and make a more subtle speech than his?

PHAEDRUS: As far as that is concerned, my friend, you have laid yourself open to the same manoeuvre you applied to me. You absolutely must deliver the best speech you can, so c that we aren't forced to trade words in the vulgar fashion of a comedy. Be careful:† I'm sure you don't want to force me to say things like 'I tell you, Socrates, if I don't know Socrates, I'm a stranger to myself too,' and 'He wanted to make the speech, but he coyly pretended he didn't.'* No, you should realize that we aren't going to leave here until you've delivered the speech you said you had in your breast. We're alone in an isolated spot, and I'm younger and stronger than you. Faced with all this, you had better 'hearken well to d what I say'* and not choose being compelled to speak rather than doing so of your own free will.

SOCRATES: The trouble is, my dear Phaedrus, I'll just make a fool of myself if I extemporize a speech on the same topic. After all, I'm a mere amateur, and I'll be compared with an expert author.

PHAEDRUS: Do you see how things stand? Stop playing hard to get. I'm pretty sure I know what to say to force you to deliver a speech.

SOCRATES: Then don't say it!

PHAEDRUS: No, I will—and it will be in the form of an oath. I swear to you—hmm, which of the gods shall I swear by? Do you mind if I take this plane tree here?—that unless e you make the speech for me, in the presence of this tree, I shall neither recite nor report for you anyone's speech ever again.

SOCRATES: Ah, you foul creature! You've certainly found a good way to make a speech-loving man do what you want.

PHAEDRUS: Then why are you trying to wriggle out of it?

SOCRATES: I'll stop, now that you've sworn this oath. How could I cut myself off from such a feast?

237a PHAEDRUS: Speak, then.

SOCRATES: Do you know what I'll do?

PHAEDRUS: In what respect?

SOCRATES: I shall cover my head* as I speak, so that I can get through my speech as quickly as possible and not be put off by embarrassment if I catch your eye.

PHAEDRUS: I don't care what else you do, just so long as you get on with your speech.

SOCRATES: Come, then, clear-voiced Muses, whether you have gained this epithet because of the quality of your singing or because the Ligurians are so musical,* 'grant me your support'* in the tale which my excellent friend here is forcing me to tell, because he wants to regard his friend as even
b more skilful and clever than he already does.

Once upon a time there was a boy, or rather a young man, who was very beautiful, and he had a great many lovers. One of these lovers was a cunning man, and although he was in love with the boy as much as anyone, he had convinced him that he was not.* The time came when, in order to try to seduce the boy, he set about persuading him of precisely this point, that he should gratify a non-lover rather than a lover. And this is what he said:

'Whatever the issue, my young friend, if you want to come to a correct conclusion there is only one place to start your
c deliberations. If you lack knowledge of whatever it is you are thinking about, you are bound to go wrong. Now, most people fail to appreciate their ignorance of the true nature of any given thing, proceed on the assumption that they do know, and end up paying the penalty you'd expect, of agreeing neither with themselves nor with anyone else. I don't want you and me to experience what we criticize in others. No, because the issue before us is whether one should enter into a relationship with a lover or a non-lover, we should establish a mutually acceptable definition of love—of what kind of thing it is, and what its
d powers are—and then we can conduct our enquiry into

16

whether it is beneficial or harmful with this definition before us as a benchmark and a point of reference.

'Well, then, it is clear to everyone that love is a kind of desire, and we also know that even non-lovers desire the beauty in people and things. So how shall we tell a lover from a non-lover? We must next bear in mind that in each of us there are two ruling and guiding forces whose lead we follow: one is our innate desire for pleasures, and the other is an acquired mode of thought, which aims for what is best. These two forces in us sometimes work together, but sometimes conflict, and at different times one or the other of them is in command. e When thought is in command and is leading us rationally towards what is best, the name we give to its rule is self-control. When desire is in command and is dragging us irrationally towards pleasures, we call its rule excess. Now, 238a excess has many names, because it is a thing of many limbs and parts, and a person in its grip gains an ugly, pejorative name according to which of the many types of excess happens to dominate at the time. When the desire for food conquers one's reasoning about what is best and overpowers the other desires, it is called gluttony and someone in its grip gains exactly that b name. Or again, when someone is ruled by the desire for alcohol and is led in that direction, we all know what name he gains for himself. And so on: in the case of all the related names of these and related desires, we can easily see that people are called by the appropriate name, depending on whichever desire is in control. We are already more or less in a position to understand the desire which all these preliminaries were leading up to, but it is always clearer to have something openly stated rather than leaving it implicit. So when irrational desire rules one's reasoned impulse to do right and is carried towards pleasure in beauty, and when this irrational desire has also been powerfully reinforced in its attraction towards physical beauty by the desires that are related to it, and has gained the c upper hand thanks to this power, it is named after that very strength, and is called love.'*

Anyway, my dear Phaedrus, do you think I've been inspired by a god? I do.*

PHAEDRUS: Well, it's certainly true that you're being unusually eloquent, Socrates.*

SOCRATES: Keep quiet and listen to me, then. For in fact this spot really does seem infused with divinity, so don't be sur-
d prised if, as may happen, I become possessed by the Nymphs* as my speech progresses. As it is I'm already more or less chanting dithyrambs.*

PHAEDRUS: You're quite right.

SOCRATES: It's your fault. But listen to the rest of the speech. After all, the fit might be averted, I suppose. But we had better leave this in the hands of the gods, while we resume the speech to the boy.

'All right, then, brave heart.* Now that we have stated and defined the matter we have to think about, we can refer to it in
e what follows and say what benefit or damage is likely to accrue from a lover or a non-lover to the person who gratifies either of them. A man who is ruled by desire and is a slave to pleasure is surely bound to see to it that his beloved gives him as much pleasure as possible. Now, someone who is sick finds pleasant only things which offer him no resistance, while he hates any-thing which is stronger than him, or just as strong as him. So a
239a lover will not be happy with a beloved who is superior to him, or his equal, and he will always try to make him weaker and inferior. Now, a stupid person is inferior to a clever one, a cowardly person is inferior to a brave one, one who finds it impossible to speak in public is inferior to an orator, and a dull-witted person is inferior to a quick-witted one. A lover is bound to find pleasant the occurrence and the natural presence in his beloved of not just these terrible afflictions, but even more besides, and he will make sure that his beloved has them, so as not to risk losing his short-term pleasure. He is bound to be jealous, then, and because he stops him entering into a
b number of other beneficial relationships, which might have

18

gone a long way towards developing his potential, he is bound
to harm him a great deal, and a very great deal if he denies him
the kind of relationship which would develop his intellectual
capacities. This, in fact, would come about from the divine
pursuit, philosophy,* which a lover is bound to keep his beloved
far away from, for fear of finding himself an object of contempt. And in general he will ensure that his beloved remains
utterly ignorant and utterly dependent on him, in which state
the beloved will give the greatest pleasure to his lover, but do
the greatest harm to himself. Anyway, as far as the mind is
concerned, there is no advantage at all in having as your c
guardian and partner a man who is in love.

'Next we must turn to your physical state and care of the
body, and try to see how and in what way a man who is compelled to make pleasure rather than goodness his goal will treat
a body which he is in charge of. You will soon see that he
chases after someone who is soft, not hard, someone who has
been brought up in hazy shade rather than in the pure light of
the sun and who has no experience of manly toil and dried
sweat, but has plenty of experience of a comfortable and
effeminate way of life, someone who prettifies himself with
alien colours and make-up* because he has none of his own, d
and whose other pursuits are all in keeping with those we
have already mentioned. They are obvious and there is nothing to be gained by adding to the list, but we can move on
once we have briefly stated the main point: in times of war
and other important crises, a body of this kind encourages
your enemies and dismays your friends and even your lovers
themselves.

'All this is too obvious to need saying, but next it does need
to be asked what benefit or harm the company and protection e
of a lover will do as far as possessions are concerned. Now, if
there is anything of which everyone, but especially a lover, is
aware it is that he would pray above all else for his beloved to
lose his most precious, kind, and divine possessions. For he
would gladly see him deprived of his father, mother, relatives,

and friends, whom he regards as obstacles to and critics of
240a what gives him the greatest pleasure—spending time with his
beloved. Also, in his opinion, the possession of gold or other
valuables makes a boy less easy to catch, and less tame when
caught, and from this it clearly follows that a lover hates it
when his beloved has possessions, and loves to see him lose
them. Then again, a lover would pray for his beloved to be
without wife, children, and home for as long as possible,
because he wants to spend as long as possible plucking the
fruit he finds sweet.

'There are plenty of other evils, but thanks to some deity or
other most of them do involve short-term pleasure. Take a
b parasite, for example: he is a formidable creature and a source
of considerable harm, but he naturally involves a not unrefined
kind of pleasure.* Again, although one might criticize prosti-
tutes as harmful, along with many other such creatures and
pursuits, they are very enjoyable, in an ephemeral fashion. Not
only does a lover harm his beloved, however, but there is no
pleasure at all to be had in his company. After all, as the old
c saying says, youth pleases youth*—presumably because people
of the same age have the same pleasures and this similarity
makes them friends—but one can see too much even of one's
peers.

'Furthermore, in every walk of life pressure is a nuisance for
anyone. And apart from the difference in their ages a lover
exerts enormous pressure on his beloved. For in such a relationship the older man is reluctant to leave the younger at any
time of the day or night; he is driven by compulsion, stung by
d a goad which, by constantly giving him pleasure when he sees,
hears, touches, or otherwise perceives his beloved, induces him
to find pleasure in being the boy's attentive servant. But what
kind of consolation or pleasure can he offer his beloved to stop
him being absolutely disgusted by spending all that time with
him? He sees a face which is aged and past its prime, and
everything else that goes with that, which it is unpleasant even
e to hear about, let alone being pressurized into experiencing the

actuality of it. He is watched constantly and suspiciously in all his dealings with other people, he listens to excessive and inappropriate praise and to the same sort of criticism, which is intolerable when his lover is sober, and embarrassing as well as intolerable when he is drunk and talks with tiresome and unrestrained candour.

'A lover in love damages and disgusts his beloved, but once he has fallen out of love he is no longer to be trusted, for all the promises he made about the future, and for all the oaths and entreaties with which he accompanied those promises, as a barely successful ploy to offset the arduous nature of his company with the hope of advantages to come and so have his 241a beloved stay with him for the time being. Later, then, when he ought to be fulfilling these promises, he swaps one internal ruler and master for another, and listens to sanity and common sense rather than love and madness. His beloved, however, does not realize that he has changed; he demands kindness from him in return for favours granted earlier, and reminds him of things he did and said, as if he were talking to the same man. The lover, meanwhile, is too embarrassed to admit that he has changed, and is also incapable of fulfilling the oaths and promises of the earlier, insane regime, because he has now come to his senses and recovered his sanity, and does not want b to turn back into the same person he was before as a result of doing the same things as then. And so he tries to flee his responsibilities. Compelled to default by the change he has undergone, the former lover, at the flip of a sherd,* turns to flight. The beloved is then forced to chase after him,* cursing in his frustration, and completely and utterly failing to appreciate that he should never gratify someone who is in love and who is bound to be out of his mind, but would do much better to gratify someone who is not in love with him and is sane. c Otherwise, he is bound to be surrendering himself to a man who is untrustworthy, bad-tempered, jealous, unpleasant, and harmful not just to his property and his physical condition, but even more so to his mental development, which is in actual fact the most valuable thing there is or ever will be in the eyes of both gods and men.

'All this, then, young man, is what you have to bear in mind. You should realize that kindness is not involved in a relationship with a lover. For him it is like food, just so that he can be
d filled up. Lovers love a young man like yourself as wolves love lambs!'*

That's it, Phaedrus. I have nothing to add to what I've said, and you must take my speech as ended.

PHAEDRUS: But I thought you were only halfway through, and would talk at the same length about the non-lover— about how it is preferable for the boy to gratify him—and would explain all the advantages he brings. But you seem to have stopped, Socrates. Why?

e SOCRATES: Didn't you notice, my friend, that I've stopped chanting dithyrambs and am now coming up with epic verse, even though I'm finding fault with things?* So what do you think would happen if I set about praising the non-lover? Don't you realize that I'd certainly be possessed by the Nymphs to whom you have deliberately exposed me? I shall say only, in a word, that the non-lover has all the advantages opposed to the attributes we criticized in the lover. So what need is there of a long speech? I've said enough about them both. In this situation the tale I have told will meet with the appropriate fate, and I am going
242a to cross this river and leave before you force me to do something even worse.

PHAEDRUS: Not yet, Socrates—not while it's so hot. Can't you see that it's almost midday now—the dead time of day, as it is called? No, we should wait and talk about the speeches, and leave presently, when it cools down.

SOCRATES: You are extraordinary when it comes to speeches, Phaedrus—quite remarkable. I should think that if we were to consider all the speeches that have been composed during your lifetime, we would find that you were responsible for

more of them than anyone else, either because you delivered b
them yourself or because by fair means or foul you forced
others to do so.* Leaving aside Simmias of Thebes, you easily beat everyone else. And I think that now you're proving
once again to be responsible for the delivery of a speech.

PHAEDRUS: That's good news, but what do you mean? What
is this speech you're referring to?

SOCRATES: I was just about to cross the river, my friend, when
my familiar divine sign came to me, which stops me from
time to time when I'm about to do something.* I seemed to c
hear a sudden voice telling me not to leave until I have
purified myself from some offence or other which I have
committed against the realm of the gods. Now, I may not be
a very good one, but I am a seer. I'm like people who are bad
at writing: I'm good enough only for my own purposes. And
so I do already understand beyond the shadow of a doubt
what my offence was. After all, the soul too has something
of the same ability that seers possess. Just now, when I was
delivering my speech, something disturbed me, and I was
rather worried, as Ibycus says, 'lest the cost of winning honour among men is that I sin in the eyes of the gods'.* But now d
I see where I went wrong.

PHAEDRUS: And that is?

SOCRATES: It was an awful speech, Phaedrus, just awful—the
one you brought with you, and the one you forced me to
make.

PHAEDRUS: Why?

SOCRATES: It was stupid and almost irreligious, and speeches
don't come more awful than that.

PHAEDRUS: No, they don't, if you're right.

SOCRATES: Well, don't you think that Love is a god, and the
son of Aphrodite?

PHAEDRUS: That's what we're told.

SOCRATES: But that wasn't what we were told by Lysias, nor
was it in your speech,* the one for which you bewitched me
into being your mouthpiece. But if Love is a god, or at least e

23

divine,* as indeed he is, he cannot be bad, but both the speeches which have just been given about him made him out to be bad. Not only did they commit this offence against Love, but their stupidity attained exquisite heights: although everything they said was unsound and false, they gave themselves solemn airs as if they were important, to see
243a   if they could deceive some pathetic people into admiring them. And so I must purify myself, my friend. Now, there's an ancient tradition governing how those who commit an offence in the domain of story-telling have to purify themselves, which Homer may have failed to recognize, but Stesichorus didn't.* After losing his sight as a result of slandering Helen, Stesichorus didn't fail to recognize his fault, as Homer had. No, as a man of culture he recognized how he had sinned and immediately composed the following lines:

> False was the tale I told.
> You did not travel on the fair-decked ship,
b   > Nor came to the citadel of Troy.*

And no sooner had he finished composing the entire *Palinode*, as it is called, than he regained his sight. Well, I shall prove myself cleverer than them in one respect, anyway: I shall try to recompense Love with my palinode before anything happens to me as a result of slandering him, and I shall not keep my head covered out of embarrassment as I did before, but shall speak with my head exposed.

PHAEDRUS: You couldn't have said anything which would make me happier, Socrates.

c SOCRATES: That, my dear Phaedrus, is because you're aware how shameless the two speeches were, the one given just now and the one read out from the scroll. I mean, if we'd been overheard by anyone of breeding and gentility who either was or had been in love with someone like himself, and if he'd heard us saying that trivial incidents provoke violent hostilities in men who are in love, and that their attitude towards their beloveds is governed by jealousy and guaranteed to be harmful, don't you think he'd inevitably assume that he was listening to people who'd been brought up among sailors and had never witnessed non-slavish love? Don't you think he'd totally disagree with our criticisms of d Love?

PHAEDRUS: Yes, Socrates, he certainly might.

SOCRATES: Out of respect for him, then, and fear of Love himself, I want to wash away the unpleasant taste, so to speak, of these two speeches with a fresh one. And I'd recommend Lysias too to compose a speech as soon as he can about how one should gratify a lover rather than a non-lover in return for favours received.

PHAEDRUS: That will happen, I assure you. Once you've made a speech in praise of a lover, I'll stop at absolutely nothing to get Lysias to compose the same kind of e speech.

SOCRATES: I'm sure he will, given that you are who you are.

PHAEDRUS: So you don't need to worry. Just give your speech.

SOCRATES: Where's that boy I was talking to before? I want him to hear the speech too, and not to rush off and gratify a non-lover without having heard what I have to say.

PHAEDRUS: He's always right here by your side, whenever you need him.

SOCRATES: What I'd like you to realize, you gorgeous young man, is that the previous speech was by Phaedrus the son of Pythocles, of the deme Myrrhinous,* and that the one 244a I'm just about to give will be by Stesichorus the son of Euphemus, from Himera.* Here's what I have to say:

'"False was the tale"* that you should gratify a non-lover rather than a lover (supposing you have one), just because a lover is mad and a non-lover is sane. If madness were simply an evil, it would be right, but in fact some of our greatest blessings come from madness, when it is granted to us as a

25

divine gift. For instance, the prophetess at Delphi and the priestesses at Dodona* have done Greece a lot of good—not
b only individuals, but whole communities—in their madness, but little or nothing when they are in their right minds. And if we are to mention the Sibyl* and all the others who, when possessed by a god, use prophecy to predict the future and have on numerous occasions pointed a lot of people in the right direction, we would only be lengthening our account with information that was already completely familiar.

'But it is worth mentioning as evidence that the people who made up our language long ago were also of the opinion that madness was not appalling or disgraceful. Otherwise they would not have linked this word, "madness", with the wonder-
c ful art of foretelling the future by calling it "insanity" [manikē]. No, they gave this wonderful art its name on the assumption that madness is fine, when it comes from divine dispensation, but people nowadays are ignorant of such nuances and so they insert the "t" and call it "prophecy" [man-tikē].* By the same token, when they named the investigation of the future by people who are in their right minds,† which is carried out by means of birds and other signs, they called it "augury" [oionoïstikē] because it gives the human mind [oiēsis] insight [nous] and information [historia] in a rational way, although nowadays people call it oiōnistikē to make it sound
d more special with a long "o". So, because prophecy is more complete and valuable than augury—not just because it has a superior name, but also because its achievements are superior —those men of old were indicating that god-given madness is better than human sanity.

'Then again, madness enters certain famous families which have been afflicted by horrendous illnesses and suffering as a result of guilt incurred some time in the distant past,* and with prophetic insight finds the necessary means of relief. It resorts
e to prayer and worship of the gods, and when, as a result of this, it comes up with purificatory rituals, it makes the madman better, not just temporarily, but for the future too. And so it

finds a way to release people who are mad and possessed in the right fashion from the evils that afflict them.

'A third kind of possession and madness comes from the 245a Muses.* It takes hold of a delicate, virgin soul and stirs it into a frenzy for composing lyric and other kinds of poetry, and so educates future generations by glorifying the countless deeds of the past. But anyone who approaches the doors of poetic composition without the Muses' madness, in the conviction that skill alone will make him a competent poet, is cheated of his goal. In his sanity both he and his poetry are eclipsed by poetry composed by men who are mad.

'So there are some examples of the fine results of god-sent b madness; I could mention even more as well. And the upshot is that we should not be afraid of madness, and should not be alarmed by the argument, designed to frighten us, that we should prefer a sane man over a passionate one as our friend. This argument can win the day only if it can also show that love is not sent by the gods to benefit the lover and his beloved. Meanwhile, it is up to us to prove, on the contrary, that this kind of madness* is given by the gods to help us achieve the greatest happiness—a proof which will be believed by the wise, c if not the clever.

'First we have to understand the truth about the nature of the soul,* whether divine or human, by considering what happens to it and what it causes to happen. This gives us the following starting-point for our proof. Every soul is immortal,* because anything that is ever-moving is immortal, whereas anything which causes motion elsewhere and is moved from elsewhere stops living when it stops moving. It is only something which moves itself that never stops moving, because it never abandons itself.† Such a thing is also the original source of motion for everything else that moves. Now, a source is ungenerated, because everything that is generated is necessar- d ily generated from a source, but there is nothing for a source to be generated from. For if a source were generated from anything, it would stop being a source. Since a source is ungenerated, it is also necessarily imperishable, because a defunct source can never be generated from anything else nor can it bring about generation in anything else, given that everything is generated from a source. And so it is a self-mover that is a source of motion, and a self-mover can neither perish nor be generated, or else the entire universe and the whole of e creation† will inevitably run down and stop, and will never again find anything to act as a source of motion and generation. Now, we have already shown that a self-mover is immortal, and so no one need hesitate to claim that self-movement is the essence and principle of soul.* For no body which is moved from outside itself has a soul, while every body which is moved from within itself, from its own resources, has a soul, since this is what it is to be soul. If this is so—if souls 246a and only souls are self-movers—it necessarily follows that soul is ungenerated and immortal.

'That is enough about the soul's immortality. I must now say something about its character. It would take too long—and beyond the slightest shadow of a doubt require a god—to explain its character, but the use of an analogy will make the task within lesser human powers. So let's do that. In my analogy, a soul is like an organic whole made up of a charioteer and his team of horses.* Now, while the horses and charioteers of gods are always thoroughly good, those of everyone else are b a mixture.* Although our inner ruler drives a pair of horses, only one of his horses is thoroughly noble and good, while the other is thoroughly the opposite. This inevitably makes driving, in our case, difficult and disagreeable.

'Next I must try to explain how one living creature is called "immortal" while another is called "mortal".* It is the job of soul in general to look after all that is inanimate,* and souls patrol the whole universe, taking on different forms at different times. A complete soul—which is to say, one that is winged c —journeys on high and controls the whole world, but one that has lost its wings is carried along until it seizes upon something solid, and it takes up residence there. The earthy body of which it takes control seems to move itself, but that is the effect of the soul, and the whole unit of soul and body conjoined is called a "living creature", and also "mortal". No one who has thought the matter through could call a living creature "immortal", but because we have never seen a god, and have an inadequate conception of godhood, we imagine a kind of immortal living creature, possessing both soul and body in an everlasting combination. Anyway, we can leave the facts of this matter to be and be expressed however the gods like, but we have to come to some understanding of what causes a soul to shed and lose its wings. It is something like this.

'The natural property of a wing is to carry something heavy aloft, up on high to the abode of the gods. There is a sense in which, of all the things that are related to the body, wings have more of the divine in them. Anything divine is good, wise, virtuous, and so on, and so these qualities are the best source of nourishment and growth for the soul's wings, but badness and evil and so on cause them to shrink and perish.

'The supreme leader in the heavens is Zeus. He goes at the head, in a winged chariot, arranging and managing everything, and behind him comes the host of gods and spirits, in an orderly array of eleven squadrons.* For Hestia stays alone in the gods' house, while each of the other gods who have been assigned one of the twelve positions takes his place at the head of the rank to which he has been assigned. So there are many glorious sights to be seen within heaven, and many wonderful paths along which the favoured company of gods go and return, each performing his proper function,* and the gods are accompanied by everyone who wants to join them and is capable of doing so, because meanness has no place in the gods' choir. When they turn to food and go to one of their banquets, they journey skyward to the rim of the heavenly vault. Although the way is steep, the gods' chariots make light of the journey, since they are well balanced and easy to handle, but the other chariots find it hard, because the troublesome horse weighs them down. Any charioteer who has trained this horse

d

e

247a

b

imperfectly finds that it pulls him down towards the earth and holds him back, and this is the point at which a soul faces the worst suffering and the hardest struggle.

'When the souls we call "immortal"* reach the rim, they make their way to the outside and stand on the outer edge of
c heaven, and as they stand there the revolution carries them around, while they gaze outward from the heaven. The region beyond heaven has never yet been adequately described in any of our earthly poets' compositions, nor will it ever be. But since one has to make a courageous attempt to speak the truth, especially when it is truth that one is speaking about, here is a description. This region is filled with true being. True being has no colour or form; it is intangible, and visible only to intelligence, the soul's guide. True being is the province of
d everything that counts as true knowledge. So since the mind of god is nourished by intelligence and pure knowledge (as is the mind of every soul which is concerned to receive its proper food), it is pleased to be at last in a position to see true being, and in gazing on the truth it is fed and feels comfortable, until the revolution carries it around to the same place again. In the course of its circuit it observes justice as it really is, self-control, knowledge—not the kind of knowledge that is involved with change and differs according to which of the
e various existing things (to use the term "existence" in its everyday sense) it makes its object, but the kind of knowledge whose object is things as they really are. And once it has feasted its gaze in the same way on everything else that really is, it sinks back into the inside of heaven and returns home.* Once back home, the soul's charioteer reins in his horses by their manger, throws them ambrosia to eat, and gives them nectar to wash the ambrosia down.*

248a   'This is how the gods live. As for the other souls, any that have closely followed a god and have come to resemble him most* raise the heads of their charioteers into the region outside and are carried around along with the revolution, but they are disturbed by their horses and their view of things as they really are is uncertain. Others poke their heads through from time to time, but sink back down in between, and so they see some things, but miss others, depending on the resistance offered by their horses. The rest all long for the upper region and follow after, but they cannot break through, and they are carried around under the surface, trampling and bumping into one another as one tries to overtake another. So there is utter b chaos, nothing but sweat and conflict. In the course of this confusion many souls are crippled as a result of the incompetence of the charioteers, and many have their wings severely damaged, but even after all this effort none of them succeeds in seeing things as they really are before having to return and rely on specious nourishment.*

'The reason why there is so much determination to see the whereabouts of the plain of truth* is not only that the proper food for the best part of the soul happens to come from the meadow there, but also that it is in the nature of the wings c which raise the soul to be nourished by this region. It is the decree of destiny that any soul which attends a god and catches even a glimpse of the truth remains free from injury until the next revolution, and if it is able to do this every time, it will continue to be free from harm. But souls which fall behind and lose their vision of the truth, and are for some unfortunate reason or another weighed down by being filled with forgetfulness and weakness, lose their wings thanks to this burden and fall to earth. At this point they are subject to a law that they are not to be planted into the bodies of animals in their first incar- d nation. The souls which have seen the most are to enter the seeds of men who will become philosophers, lovers of beauty, men of culture, men who are dedicated to love;* the second group those of law-abiding kings or military commanders or civic leaders; the third group those of politicians, estate-managers or businessmen; the fourth group those of men who love exercising in a gymnasium† or future experts in bodily health; the fifth group will live as prophets or as initiators into one of the mystery cults;* the sixth group will most suitably

e live as poets or some other kind of representative artist, the
seventh as artisans or farmers, the eighth as sophists or
demagogues, and the ninth as tyrants.*

'In all these cases anyone who has lived a moral life will
obtain a better fate, and anyone who has lived an immoral life
the opposite.* For no soul returns to the place it fell from for
ten thousand years*—it takes that long for wings to grow again

249a —except the soul of a man who has practised philosophy with
sincerity or combined his love for a boy with the practice of
philosophy. At the completion of the third thousand-year circuit, if these souls have chosen the philosophical life three
times in succession, they regain their wings and in the three-
thousandth year they return.* But all the other souls are judged
after the end of their first life, and once they have been judged
they either go to prisons in the underworld where they are
punished, or are raised aloft by Justice to a certain place in the
heavens and live as they deserve, depending on how they lived

b when they were in human form.* But in the thousandth year
both groups of souls come for the allotment and choice of their
second life and each of them chooses the life it likes.* This is
the point at which a human soul can be reincarnated as an
animal, and someone who was formerly human can be reborn
as a human being once again, instead of being an animal. For a
soul which has never seen the truth cannot enter into human
form, because a man must understand the impressions he
receives† by reference to classes: he draws on the plurality of

c perceptions to combine them by reasoning into a single class.
This is recollection of the things which our souls once saw
during their journey as companions to a god, when they saw
beyond the things we now say "exist" and poked their heads
up into true reality.* That is why only the mind of a philosopher deserves to grow wings, because it uses memory to
remain always as close as possible to those things proximity to
which gives a god his divine qualities. By making correct use of
reminders of these things a man, being constantly initiated
into the most perfect rites of all, becomes the only one who is

truly perfect. But since he is remote from human concerns and close to divinity, he is criticized by the general run of mankind d as deranged, because they do not realize that he is possessed by a god.

'Now we reach the point to which the whole discussion of the fourth kind of madness was tending. This fourth kind of madness is the kind which occurs when someone sees beauty here on earth and is reminded of true beauty. His wings begin to grow and he wants to take to the air on his new plumage, but he cannot; like a bird he looks upwards, and because he ignores what is down here, he is accused of behaving like a madman.* So the point is that this turns out to be the most thoroughly e good of all kinds of possession, not only for the man who is possessed, but also for anyone who is touched by it,* and the word "lover" refers to a lover of beauty who has been possessed by this kind of madness.* For, as I have already said, the soul of every human being is bound to have seen things as they really are, or else it would not have entered this kind of living creature.

'But not every soul is readily prompted by things here on 250a earth to recall those things that are real. This is not easy for souls which caught only a brief glimpse of things there, nor for those which after falling to earth have suffered the misfortune of being perverted and made immoral by the company they keep and have forgotten the sacred things they saw then. When the remaining few, whose memories are good enough, see a likeness here which reminds them of things there, they are amazed and beside themselves, but they do not understand what is happening to them because of a certain unclarity in their perceptions. But although the likenesses here on earth (of things which are precious to souls, such as justice and self- b control) lack all lustre, and only a few people come to them and barely see, through dim sense organs, what it is that any likeness is a likeness of, yet earlier it was possible for them to see beauty in all its brilliance. That was when—we as attendants of Zeus* and others of one of the other gods—as part of a happy

33

company they saw a wonderful sight and spectacle and were
initiated into what we may rightly call the most wonderful of
c the mysteries. When we celebrated these mysteries then, we
were not only perfect beings ourselves, untouched by all the
troubles which awaited us later, but we also were initiated into
and contemplated things shown to us that were perfect, simple, stable, and blissful. We were surrounded by rays of pure
light, being pure ourselves and untainted by this object we call
a "body" and which we carry around with us now, imprisoned
like shellfish.*

'Let this be my tribute to memory; it was remembering and
longing for those past events which has made me go on rather
too long now.* But turning to beauty, it shone out, as I said,
d among its companions there, and once here on earth we found,
by means of the clearest of our senses, that it sparkles with
particular clarity. For the keenest kind of perception the body
affords us is the one that comes through seeing, though we are
not able to see wisdom, because as with everything else which
is an object of love,† wisdom would cause terrible pangs of
love in us if it presented some kind of clear image of itself by
approaching our organ of sight. But as things are, it is only
beauty which has the property of being especially visible and
e especially lovable.* Anyone who was initiated long ago or who
has been corrupted is not given to moving rapidly from here to
there, towards beauty as it really is. Instead, he gazes on its
namesake here on earth, and the upshot is that the sight does
not arouse reverence in him. No, he surrenders to pleasure and
tries like an animal to mount his partner and to father offspring, and having become habituated to excess he is not afraid
251a or ashamed to pursue unnatural pleasures.* But when someone
who has only recently been initiated, and who took in plenty of
the sights to be seen then, sees a marvellous face or a bodily
form which is a good reflection of beauty, at first he shivers
and is gripped by something like the fear he felt then, and the
sight also moves him to revere his beloved as if he were a god.
In fact, it is only concern about being thought completely

insane that stops him from sacrificing to his beloved as if he were a cult statue or a god.*

'Following this sight, the kind of change comes over him that you would expect after a shivering fit, and he begins to sweat and to run an unusually high fever, because the reception through his eyes of the effusion of beauty causes him to b get hot. Now, this effusion is also the natural means of irrigating his wings. His heat softens the coat covering the feathers' buds, which had been too hard and closed up for wings to grow. As further nourishment pours in, the quills of the feathers swell and begin to grow from the roots upwards and to spread all over the under side of the soul, because previously the whole soul was winged. At this point, then, his whole soul seethes and pounds—in fact, the soul of someone who is c beginning to grow wings experiences exactly the same sensations that children feel when they are teething, with their teeth just starting to grow, and they feel an itching and a soreness in their gums. So the soul, as it grows its wings, seethes and feels sore and tingles.

'When it gazes on the young man's beauty, and receives the particles emanating from it as they approach and flow in— which, of course, is why we call it desire*—it is watered and heated, and it recovers from its pain and is glad. But when it is away from the boy and becomes parched, the dryness makes d the mouths of the channels for the budding feathers close up and contain the wings' new growth. The new shoots are shut up inside along with the desire. They throb like pulsing veins, and each one rubs against its channel, with the result that the whole soul stings all over and is frantic with pain—until it remembers the boy in his beauty and is glad. The strange sensation of mingled pain and pleasure is agony for it, and its helplessness torments it. It is too disturbed to sleep at night or e stay still by day, and it rushes around to wherever it thinks it might see the boy who bears the beauty it longs for. The sight of him opens the irrigation channels of desire and frees the former blockage; it finds relief and an end to the stinging pain,

35

and once more enjoys this, for the time being, as the most
252a intense pleasure. This is not something it willingly does without, and it values no one more than the beautiful boy. It is
oblivious to mothers, brothers, and all its friends. It does not
care in the slightest if its wealth suffers through neglect. It
despises all the customs and good manners on which it had
previously prided itself. Indeed, it is ready to play the part of a
slave and to sleep wherever it is allowed to, as long as it is as
close as possible to the object of its desire. For as well as
worshipping the boy who bears the beauty, it has discovered
b that he is also the only one who can cure it of its terrible
suffering.

'This, you beautiful boy, to whom I am addressing this
speech—this is the experience men call love, but you are
probably too young to think of what the gods call it as anything
but a joke. I think that some Homeric scholars recite two
verses from the unpublished poems of Homer which have to
do with Love. The second of the two verses is quite outra-
geous and not very metrical at all. The couplet goes like this:

> He is the winged one that mortals call "Eros",
> But since he must grow wings the gods call him "Pteros".*

c You can believe this or not, as you wish. But at any rate the
background to and experience of being in love are as I have
said.

'Now, if the captive is one of the attendants of Zeus, he can
endure the burden of the Winged One with some dignity. But
things are different when the servants of Ares, who made the
circuitous journey in his company, are captured by Love. If
they have the slightest inkling that they have been wronged by
their beloved, they become murderous: they are quite ready to
immolate both themselves and their beloveds. And so it goes
for every single god: as long as he has not yet been corrupted
and is living the first of his lives here on earth, an individual
spends his life honouring and imitating to the best of his abil-
d ity the god to whose chorus he belongs, and in all his dealings

and relations, including his love-affairs, he conforms to this mode of behaviour. So which good-looking boy an individual chooses as his beloved† depends on his disposition, and he treats the boy as if he were that very god: he constructs for himself an image, so to speak, and decorates it in order to worship his god and celebrate his rites.

'The followers of Zeus, then, want someone with a Zeus- e like soul as their beloved. They look for someone with the potential to be a philosopher and a leader, and when they find him and have fallen in love with him, they do all they can to develop this potential in him. If they have not undertaken such a task before, they set about it now, by learning from any available sources and searching by themselves. In hunting on 253a their own for the nature of their god they are helped by the intense compulsion they are under of gazing on the god.* Since they are in contact with the god in their memories, they are inspired by him and, in so far as it is possible for a mortal man to partake of a god, they derive their way of life and the things they do from him. And because they hold their beloved responsible for this, they feel even more affection for him, and as if Zeus were a well from which they draw water, Bacchant-like* they pour it over their beloved's soul and make him as similar to their own god as they can.

'Those who were in Hera's company, on the other hand, b look for a boy with kingly qualities, and when they find him they behave in exactly the same way with him. And the follow-ers of Apollo and each of the other gods proceed in the same way, in accordance with the nature of their god, and look for a boy for themselves who has the same qualities as themselves.* When they find him, they not only imitate the god themselves, but also, by means of persuasion and attunement, they get the boy to conform, as much as he can, to the god's way of life and characteristics. There is no malice or mean-spirited ill-will in their dealings with their beloveds.* No, they behave as they do because they are trying their utmost to get the boy completely and utterly to resemble themselves and the god to whom they c are dedicated. What true lovers are committed to, the consummation of their quest†—at any rate, if they attain their goal in the way I have been describing—thus becomes admirable and a way for someone who is maddened by love to secure the happiness of the object of his affection, if he captures him.

'I will now describe how a captive is caught. Let's stick to the threefold division of the soul we made at the start of this tale, with each and every soul consisting of two horse-like d aspects and a third like a charioteer. Now, we said that one of the horses was good and the other bad, but we did not describe the goodness of the good one and the badness of the bad one. We must do so now. The one in the better position* has an upright appearance, and is clean-limbed, high-necked, hooknosed, white in colour, and dark-eyed; his determination to succeed is tempered by self-control and respect for others, which is to say that he is an ally of true glory; and he needs no whip, but is guided only by spoken commands.* The other is e crooked, over-large, a haphazard jumble of limbs; he has a thick, short neck, and a flat face; he is black in colour, with grey, bloodshot eyes, an ally of excess and affectation, hairy around the ears, hard of hearing, and scarcely to be controlled with a combination of whip and goad.

'So when the charioteer sees the light of his beloved's eyes, his whole soul is suffused with a sensation of heat and he is 254a filled with the tingling and pricking of desire. The horse that is obedient to the charioteer restrains itself from leaping on its beloved, because as always it is held back by a sense of shame. The other horse, however, stops paying any attention to the charioteer's goad and whip; it prances and lunges forward violently, making life extremely difficult for its team-mate and for the charioteer, and compelling them to head towards the beloved and bring up the subject of the pleasures of sex.* At first, these two get annoyed at being forced to behave in a way b that seems dreadfully wrong, and put up some resistance, but eventually, finding no end to their troubles, they let themselves be led forward, and they passively submit to doing as they are told. And so they come close to their beloved and see the lightning-bright beauty of his face. At this sight the charioteer's memory is taken back to the nature of true beauty, and he sees it again in place on a holy pedestal, next to self-control.* The vision terrifies him and he rears back in awe—which inevitably makes him pull back on the reins as well with enough force to set both horses down on their haunches, the c one willingly because of its obedience and the unruly one with a great deal of reluctance.

'After the two horses have withdrawn some way back, the good one drenches the whole soul in sweat brought on by its shame and horror, while the other, once it has got over the pain caused by the bit and its fall, scarcely takes time to draw breath before bursting out into furious abuse and hurling curses at both the charioteer and its team-mate for being cowardly and gutless deserters and defaulters. Once more it tries to force them to approach, against their wills, but it reluctantly agrees d to their request to wait until later. When the proposed time arrives, it reminds them of their promise, while they both feign forgetfulness, and so, plunging and neighing, it forcibly drags them up to the beloved again in order to make the same suggestion to him as before. As they get close, with head lowered and tail out straight, it bites down on the bit and shamelessly drags them on. But then the same thing happens again to the charioteer, only even more strongly: he recoils as if from a trap e and even more violently wrenches the unruly horse's bit back out of its teeth, splashing its curse-laden tongue and jaws with blood, pinning its legs and haunches to the ground, and causing it pain. Once the same thing has happened to it over and over again, the bad horse calms down, and now that it has been humbled it lets itself be guided by the charioteer's intentions. Now, when it sees the good-looking boy, it is frightened to death, and the upshot is that at last the lover's soul follows his beloved in reverence and awe.*

'Not only is the boy now being treated as godlike and re- 255a ceiving every kind of service from a man who is not merely

39

pretending to be in love, but does genuinely feel it, but also it is natural for him to feel affection for someone who is treating him so well. As a result, even if previously he had been put off by the assertion of his schoolfriends or whoever that associating with a lover was wrong, and had therefore repelled his lover's advances, yet now, with the passage of time, increasing maturity induces him to allow him into his company, and he is

b compelled to do so also by necessity, in the sense that it is fated that bad men can never be friends and that good men can never fail to be friends. Once he has allowed him in and has accepted his conversation and company, experience from close at hand of the lover's good will astonishes the beloved and he realizes that the friendship of all his other friends and relatives put together does not amount to even a fraction of the friendship offered by a lover who is inspired by a god.

'When the lover has been doing this for some time, and there has been physical contact between them at meetings in

c the gymnasium and elsewhere, then at last the flowing stream (which Zeus called "desire" when he was in love with Ganymede*) pours down on the lover in such great quantities that while some of it sinks into him, the rest flows off outside as he fills up and brims over. Just as a gust of wind or an echo rebounds from smooth, hard objects and returns to where it came from, so the flow of beauty returns into the beautiful boy through his eyes, which is its natural route into the soul,† and

d when it arrives and excites him, it irrigates his wings' channels and makes his plumage start to grow, and† fills the soul of the beloved in his turn with love. So he is in love, but he has no idea what he is in love with. He does not know what has happened to him and he cannot explain it. It is as if he has caught an inflammation of the eye from someone else and cannot say where it came from;* he fails to appreciate that he is seeing himself in his lover as in a mirror. When his lover is with him, he finds just as much relief from his pain as the lover does; when his lover is not there, he misses him just as much and is missed just as much. He has contracted counter-love as

a reflection of his lover's love, but he calls it and thinks of it as e
friendship rather than love. His desires are more or less the
same as his lover's, though weaker—to see, touch, kiss, lie
down together—and as you might expect before long this is
exactly what he does.

'When they lie together, the lover's undisciplined horse
makes suggestions to the charioteer and demands a little
pleasure to reward it for all its pains. The boy's undisciplined 256a
horse has nothing to say, but in its desire and confusion
embraces the lover and kisses him. It welcomes him as someone who clearly has its best interests at heart, and when
they are lying down together it is inclined not to refuse to play
its part in gratifying any request the lover might make. Its
team-mate, however, sides with the charioteer and resists this
inclination by arguments designed to appeal to its sense of
shame. If the better aspects of their minds win and steer them
towards orderly conduct and philosophy, they live a wonderful, harmonious life here on earth, a life of self-control and b
restraint, since they have enslaved the part which allowed evil
into the soul and freed the part which allowed goodness in.
And when they die, as winged and soaring beings they have
won the first of the three truly Olympic bouts,* which brings
greater benefits than either human sanity or divine madness
can supply.

'But if they live a more ordinary life, devoted to prestige
rather than philosophy,* it is certainly possible, I imagine, that c
when they are drunk or otherwise in a careless state the two
undisciplined horses in them might find their souls
undefended and bring them together, and so that they might
choose the course which is considered the most wonderful of
all by the common run of mankind, and consummate their
relationship. Having once done so, they continue with this
course of action in the future, but not often, because what they
did was not approved by their whole minds. This pair too
spend their lives as friends (though not as close friends as the
others), not only while they are in love, but also when they

d have left love behind. They think they have exchanged vows of such enormous strength that it would be wrong for them ever to break them and fall out with each other. At the end of their lives, when they leave their bodies, they may not have any wings, but they do have the desire to gain them, and this is no small prize to have gained from the madness of love. For it is a law that those who have already made a start on the skyward journey shall no longer go into the darkness and enter upon the journey downward to the underworld. Instead, they live a life of brightness and happily travel in each other's company,

e and sooner or later, thanks to their love, gain their wings together.

'All these are the divine gifts you will gain from the friendship of a lover, young man. But since the companionship of a non-lover is tempered by human sanity, it delivers meagre and mortal rewards. It breeds in the soul of one of its friends a quality of slavishness which is commonly praised as virtue,*

257a and so makes it circle mindlessly around and under the earth for nine thousand years.*

'There you are, dear god of love. This palinode is my gift to you and my means of atonement. It was as fair and fine as I could make it, especially in its use of poetical language, as insisted on by Phaedrus.* Please forgive my earlier speech and look favourably on this one. I pray that you may be gracious and benevolent enough not to get angry and remove or impair the skill in love which you have granted me. Grant that those who are beautiful may value me even more than they already

b do. If Phaedrus and I said anything in our earlier speech which grated on you, please hold Lysias responsible, as the father of the speech, and make him stop putting words to this kind of use. Instead, have him follow his brother Polemarchus on to the path of philosophy, so that his lover here* may no longer be in two minds, as he is now, but may wholeheartedly devote his life to Love and to the language of philosophy.'

PHAEDRUS: Socrates, I too pray that this may happen, if it

really is better for Lysias and me. As for your speech, I c
found it very impressive throughout: it's so much better
constructed than your first one.* I'm rather worried, then,
that Lysias may be humiliated, if he is even prepared to
work up another speech to rival yours. The point is, you see,
my friend, that just recently a politician was rudely finding
fault with him for exactly that, and was using the term
'speech-writer' as a term of abuse throughout.* So it may be
that concern for his reputation will stop him writing
speeches.

SOCRATES: Phaedrus, you're making a fool of yourself in saying that. You badly misjudge your friend if you think he's as d
easily frightened as you suggest. But perhaps you think that
the man who was laying into him really meant all his
rudeness.

PHAEDRUS: Yes, he seemed to, Socrates. I'm sure you know as
well as I do that the people with the most power and the
highest positions in our communities are ashamed to compose speeches and let anything they themselves have written
survive, because they're worried that subsequent generations might think badly of them and call them 'sophists'.*

SOCRATES: You've forgotten about the 'sweet bend', Phaedrus.*† And apart from the bend you're forgetting just how e
much the politicians with the highest self-regard adore
speech-writing and the survival of their written works. At
any rate, they feel so much affection for those who admire
any composition of theirs that each time, at the beginning of
the piece, they inscribe the names of its admirers.

PHAEDRUS: What do you mean? I don't understand.

SOCRATES: You don't understand that the first thing to appear 258a
at the very beginning of a politician's written work† is the
name of its admirer.

PHAEDRUS: In what sense?

SOCRATES: Well, as you know, he says 'It was decreed by the
Council' or 'by the people' or by both,* and 'So-and-so proposed . . . ', which is a very pompous way for the writer to

refer to himself and sing his own praises. And then, as a way of displaying his own cleverness to his admirers, he proceeds with what he has to say and sometimes ends up with quite a long composition. How else would you describe such a piece? It's a written speech, isn't it?

b PHAEDRUS: I agree.

SOCRATES: And if this speech lasts, the author leaves the theatre* delighted, while if it is erased, so that he has nothing to do with speech-writing and isn't recognized as a writer, both he and his companions go into mourning.

PHAEDRUS: They certainly do.

SOCRATES: And this must surely be because so far from despising the practice, they actually find it wonderful.

PHAEDRUS: Of course.

SOCRATES: Well, then, once he has gained the power of
c Lycurgus or Solon or Darius, and has become a good enough politician or ruler to have achieved immortality as a speech-writer in a community, doesn't he, during his own lifetime, consider himself to be of godlike stature, and don't subsequent generations have the same opinion of him, when they contemplate his writings?*

PHAEDRUS: Certainly.

SOCRATES: Do you think, then, that any of our politicians, whoever they are and however much they dislike Lysias, tell him off for being a writer?

PHAEDRUS: No, it's unlikely, given what you're saying. They'd be criticizing their own objectives, it seems.

d SOCRATES: It's perfectly clear, then, that speech-writing is not shameful in itself.

PHAEDRUS: Yes. Why should it be?

SOCRATES: What's really shameful, though, is getting it wrong—speaking and writing shamefully badly.

PHAEDRUS: Obviously.

SOCRATES: So how does one write well or badly? Do we need to question Lysias about this, Phaedrus, or any other writer, whether he's already written anything in the past or will some time in the future, for a political or private audience, in poetic verse or in ordinary prose?

PHAEDRUS: You don't have to ask whether we need to. What e point could there possibly be to life, if it is not given by this kind of pleasure? I don't, of course, mean those pleasures whose existence depends entirely on a prior feeling of pain, which is the case with almost all physical pleasures,* and explains why it is right to call them slavish.

SOCRATES: We're not in a rush, then, apparently. Also, I think that as the cicadas sing and talk to one another in the heat above our heads, they look down on us as well. Now, if they 259a saw us behaving like most other people and spending the early afternoon dozing off under their spell as a result of mental laziness, rather than talking, it would be right for them to laugh at us. They'd think that some slaves had come to this secluded spot of theirs to have their siesta by the stream, just like sheep. But if they see us talking and sailing past them as if they were Sirens whose spell we had resisted, they might perhaps be pleased enough to give us the gift b which the gods have granted them the power to give people.

PHAEDRUS: And what gift is that? This information seems to have passed me by.*

SOCRATES: It's quite wrong for a devotee of the Muses not to have heard about this. It is said that these cicadas were once men, in the days before the Muses were born. When the Muses were born and singing had been invented, the story goes that some of the men of that time were ecstatic with pleasure, and were so busy singing that they didn't bother with food and drink, so that before they knew it they were c dead.* They were the origin of the race of cicadas, whom the Muses granted the gift of never needing any food once they were born; all they do is sing, from the moment of their births until their deaths, without eating or drinking. After dying they go to the Muses and tell them which men here on earth honoured which of them. They tell Terpsichore the names of those who have honoured her with dances and d   raise them higher in her favour; they tell Erato the names of those who have honoured her in the ways of love, and so on for all the other Muses, according to each one's area of responsibility. But they tell Calliope, the oldest of the Muses, and her companion Urania about those who spent their lives doing philosophy and honouring their particular kind of music. I should say that these two are the Muses who are especially concerned with the heavens and with the way both gods and men use words, and that there is no more beautiful sound than their voices. So there are plenty of reasons why we should talk and not fall asleep in the midday heat.*

PHAEDRUS: Let's talk, then.

e   SOCRATES: We had better look into the issue we just proposed for consideration, then—what makes speech and writing good, and what makes it bad.

PHAEDRUS: Obviously.

SOCRATES: Now, if something is going to be spoken well and properly, the mind of the speaker must know the truth of the matter to be addressed, mustn't it?

PHAEDRUS: What I've heard about this, my dear Socrates, is
260a   that it isn't essential for a would-be orator to learn what is *really* right, but only what the masses who are going to assess what he says might *take* to be right. Likewise, he doesn't need to learn what is really good or fine, but only what they think is good or fine, because that, not the truth, is the basis for persuasion.*

SOCRATES: Whatever clever people say is, of course, 'not a word to be cast aside',* Phaedrus. We must see if they have a point. Above all, we should not lightly dismiss the view you've just repeated.

PHAEDRUS: You're right.

SOCRATES: Then let's look at it like this.

PHAEDRUS: How?

b   SOCRATES: Suppose I were to persuade you to defend your-self against the enemy by getting a horse, but neither of us

46

knew what a horse was, and all I happened to have heard about you was that Phaedrus thinks a horse is the domesticated animal with the longest ears . . .

PHAEDRUS: That would be absurd, Socrates.

SOCRATES: Not yet—not until my persuasion of you began in earnest. I would compose a speech in praise of donkeys. In this speech I would call a donkey a horse, and would explain how invaluable a beast it is to have both at home and on campaign, not only because it is good for fighting from the back of, but also because it can carry baggage as well, and has a number of other uses.

c

PHAEDRUS: Now that would be absurd—totally absurd.

SOCRATES: Well, isn't it better to be an absurd friend than a formidable enemy?

PHAEDRUS: I suppose so.

SOCRATES: So suppose an orator who doesn't know about good and bad gains power in a city which is in the same state of ignorance and tries to persuade it, not by eulogizing some miserable donkey as if it were a horse, but by making bad seem good. Suppose he's carefully studied the opinions of the masses and succeeds in persuading them to act badly instead of well, what kind of crop do you think rhetoric would later harvest from the seeds it set about sowing?

d

PHAEDRUS: A rather poor one.

SOCRATES: But has our criticism of the art of speaking been unnecessarily crude, my friend? She might perhaps reply as follows: 'Incredible! What a pair of babblers you are! It's not as if I *force* people who are ignorant of the truth to learn to speak. In fact, my advice, for what it's worth, is that someone should take me up only after having grasped the truth. But the crucial point in what I'm saying is this: without me knowledge of how things really are will make no contribution at all towards expertise at persuading people.'

PHAEDRUS: And will she be right in saying this?

e

SOCRATES: I would say so, at any rate if the arguments bearing down on her support her claim to be a branch of expertise. For I seem to hear, as it were, certain arguments advancing and protesting that she is lying—that she isn't a branch of expertise at all, but an unsystematic knack.* As the Spartan said, without a grasp of truth there neither is nor ever could be genuinely professional speaking.*

261a PHAEDRUS: We need these arguments, Socrates. Bring them here to take the stand, and cross-examine them to see what they are saying and how they put it.

SOCRATES: Step forward, noble creatures, and persuade Phaedrus, the father of fair children,* that unless he practises philosophy to a sufficiently high degree of competence, he will never even get close to being a competent speaker on any topic. Let Phaedrus be the one to answer.

PHAEDRUS: Just ask your questions.

SOCRATES: All right. Wouldn't rhetoric, in general, be a kind of skilful leading of the soul* by means of words, not only in public gatherings such as the lawcourts, but also in private meetings? Isn't it the same skill whether it is dealing with slight or great issues, and something which, seen aright, is

b no more valuable when it is concerned with important matters than it is when it is dealing with trivia? Is this what you've heard about it, or what?

PHAEDRUS: No, by Zeus, I haven't heard that at all! I've heard above all of skilful speaking and writing in the context of legal cases, and skilful speaking in a political context too, but I haven't heard of any wider use.

SOCRATES: Really? Have you heard only of Nestor's and Odysseus' handbooks on skilful speaking, which the two of them composed at Troy in their spare time? Have you never heard of Palamedes' handbook?*

c PHAEDRUS: No, by Zeus, I haven't heard even of Nestor's, unless you're dressing Gorgias up as a Nestor, or perhaps Thrasymachus or Theodorus as Odysseus.

SOCRATES: Perhaps I am. Anyway, let's not pursue that. But can you tell me what the opposing parties do in lawcourts?

They make opposing speeches, don't they? What else can we say they do?

PHAEDRUS: That's it precisely.

SOCRATES: And their speeches are concerned with right and wrong, aren't they?

PHAEDRUS: Yes.

SOCRATES: Now, will someone who's skilled at this make the same people see the same thing as either right or wrong, as d he chooses?

PHAEDRUS: Of course.

SOCRATES: And when he's speaking in a political context, won't he make his fellow citizens see the same things sometimes as good, but sometimes as the opposite?

PHAEDRUS: Yes.

SOCRATES: Now, we realize, don't we, that the Eleatic Palamedes is such a skilful speaker that he makes the same things appear to his audience similar and dissimilar, or one and many, or again at rest and in motion?*

PHAEDRUS: Certainly.

SOCRATES: Then the art of arguing opposite sides of the case* is not restricted to lawcourts and the political arena. No, it seems that all speaking will be covered by a single branch of e expertise (if it really is a branch of expertise), and that it will be this skill which will enable a person to make everything conceivable similar to everything to which it is conceivably similar, and to expose another person for disguising the fact that he is making such assimilations.

PHAEDRUS: What sort of thing are you getting at?

SOCRATES: I think it will become clear if we take the following direction. Is deception more likely to happen with things which are very different, or with things which are only a little different?

PHAEDRUS: With things that are only a little different. 262a

SOCRATES: Yes, and you're more likely to get away with shifting to an opposite position if you do so gradually rather than in big leaps, aren't you?

49

PHAEDRUS: Of course.

SOCRATES: It follows that if you are to deceive someone else, while remaining undeceived yourself, you must know precisely how things resemble and differ from one another.

PHAEDRUS: That's essential.

SOCRATES: Now, if you don't know the truth of any given thing, will you be able to recognize the degree—it may be great or small—to which one unknown thing resembles another?

b PHAEDRUS: Absolutely not.

SOCRATES: So clearly it is similarities which are responsible for people being flooded by the experience of holding opinions which do not correspond to the facts—that is, of being deceived.

PHAEDRUS: Yes, that's how it happens.

SOCRATES: So is it possible for someone to be an expert at gradually getting people to change positions, by leading them by means of similarities from any given thing to its opposite, or to be good at avoiding having this done to him, if he isn't acquainted with the truth of any given thing?

PHAEDRUS: No, he'll never be able to do that.

c SOCRATES: In that case, my friend, it looks as though a person who doesn't know the truth, but has restricted his research to opinions, will come up only with a ridiculously unsystematic form of rhetorical expertise.

PHAEDRUS: It does seem so.

SOCRATES: So shall we take the speech of Lysias which you're carrying, and the speeches we delivered earlier, and look for examples of what we're calling expertise and its lack?

PHAEDRUS: That's a very good idea indeed, because at the moment our discussion is rather abstract, since it hasn't contained enough examples.

SOCRATES: Moreover, it so happens that the two speeches do
d   apparently contain an example of how someone who knows the truth can mislead his audience by playing a joke on them in the course of his speech.* For my part, Phaedrus, I can

only blame this on the local deities, and perhaps the Muses' representatives* who are singing over our heads might also have breathed this gift into us, because I certainly don't have any expertise at speaking.

PHAEDRUS: I'll take your word for it. Just explain what you're getting at.

SOCRATES: All right. Can you read me the beginning of Lysias' speech, please?

PHAEDRUS: 'You are aware of my situation and you have e heard me explain how, in my opinion, it would be to our advantage if this were to happen. I think that the fact that I happen not to be in love with you should not prevent me getting what I want. You should know that a lover regrets . . .'

SOCRATES: Stop! So we have to point out his mistakes and where his composition lacks expertise, do we?

PHAEDRUS: Yes. 263a

SOCRATES: Well, everyone recognizes that while we agree on some things, there are others we argue about.

PHAEDRUS: I think I understand what you're saying, but please could you be more explicit.

SOCRATES: When someone says the word 'iron' or 'silver', don't we all think of the same thing?

PHAEDRUS: Of course.

SOCRATES: But what about when someone says 'right' or 'good'? Isn't it the case that we all go off in different directions, and we disagree with one another and with ourselves?*

PHAEDRUS: Yes, that's right.

SOCRATES: So we agree in some cases, but not in others. b

PHAEDRUS: Yes.

SOCRATES: In which of the two kinds of case are we more easily deceived? In which of the two does rhetoric wield more power?

PHAEDRUS: Obviously in those cases where we're uncertain.

SOCRATES: So a would-be professional orator† first has to have systematically divided the two sets of words from each other, and to have grasped the distinguishing characteristic of each of the two kinds of case, the one where most people are bound to be uncertain, and the one where they are bound not to be uncertain.

c PHAEDRUS: It would be a fine intellectual achievement to have grasped this, Socrates.†

SOCRATES: And the next stage, I imagine, would be for him not to be inattentive to any instance he comes across, but to clearly perceive to which of the two categories what he's going to speak about belongs.

PHAEDRUS: Naturally.

SOCRATES: Well, now, are we to say that love belongs among the disputable cases or the straightforward ones?

PHAEDRUS: Among the disputable cases, of course. Otherwise do you think you'd have been able to talk about it as you just did? I mean, first you said that it was harmful to the beloved and the lover, and then, on the contrary, that there was nothing better than it.

d SOCRATES: You're perfectly right. Now, tell me too—I can't quite remember because of being inspired at the time— whether I defined love at the start of my speech.

PHAEDRUS: By Zeus, you certainly did, brilliantly.

SOCRATES: Well, well! How much more expertise in speeches you're attributing to the Nymphs, the daughters of Achelous, and to Pan the son of Hermes, than to Lysias the son of Cephalus! Or am I wrong? Perhaps at the beginning of his speech on love Lysias did force a particular, unique conception of love on us, just the conception he himself wanted us to gain. Perhaps he did then organize and finalize everye thing he said in the later stages of his speech with an eye on this conception of love. Shall we read the beginning of the speech again?

PHAEDRUS: If you want. But you won't find what you're looking for there.

SOCRATES: I'd like to hear the man himself, so tell me what he says.

PHAEDRUS: 'You are aware of my situation and you have heard me explain how, in my opinion, it would be to our advantage if this were to happen. I think that the fact that I happen not to be in love with you should not prevent me getting what I want. You should know that a lover regrets the favours he does once his desire comes to an end . . .' 264a

SOCRATES: He certainly seems to be nowhere near doing what we wanted to see him doing. He doesn't begin at the beginning at all, but tries to swim through his speech on his back and the wrong way round, starting at the end. He begins with what the lover would say to his beloved when he has come to the end of his speech. Or am I wrong, Phaedrus, dear heart?

PHAEDRUS: Well, Socrates, it is at any rate true that the subject of his speech is an ending.* b

SOCRATES: What about the rest of his speech? Don't you think it was all thrown together indiscriminately? Or do you think there was any real reason why what came second was put second, and so on for all the other sections of the speech? It seemed to me—but remember that I speak from a position of ignorance—that the writer just said whatever came to his mind, in a rush of generosity, but perhaps you know of some cogent principle of composition he was following in putting the passages next to one another in order in the way that he did.

PHAEDRUS: It's kind of you to think that I have the competence to tell what he was up to with so much precision. c

SOCRATES: But I'm sure you'd agree that every speech should be put together like a living creature, with its own proper body, so that it lacks neither a head nor feet. A speech should have an end and a beginning, as well as a middle, with all the parts written so that they fit in with one another and with the whole.

PHAEDRUS: Of course.

SOCRATES: Well, if you look at whether or not your friend's speech is like that, you'll be struck by how exactly it

53

resembles the epigram which some say has been inscribed on the tomb of Midas of Phrygia.

d PHAEDRUS: What is this epigram? What's the problem with it?

SOCRATES: Here it is:*

> A maid of bronze, on Midas' tomb I stand.
> As long as waters flow and trees grow grand,
> Waiting here, on tomb wet by many a tear,
> I'll tell the passer-by: Midas is buried here.

e I'm sure you can see that it makes no difference which of its lines comes first or last.

PHAEDRUS: You're making fun of Lysias' and my speech, Socrates.

SOCRATES: Well, I don't want to make you cross, so let's say no more about this speech. All the same, I do think it contains a good number of examples which one could profitably look at, although one would certainly not profit from trying to imitate them. Still, let's turn to the other speeches, because there's something about them which, I think, bears examination by anyone who wants to investigate speeches.

265a PHAEDRUS: What are you getting at?

SOCRATES: That in a sense they took up opposite positions. One of them claimed that one should gratify a lover, the other a non-lover.

PHAEDRUS: They did, and very manfully too.

SOCRATES: I thought you were going to say 'and very *madly* too', which would have been no less than the truth, and was exactly what I had in mind. After all, we did say that love was a kind of madness, didn't we?

PHAEDRUS: Yes.

SOCRATES: But there are two kinds of madness, one caused by human illnesses, the other by a divine release from the norms of conventional behaviour.

b PHAEDRUS: Quite so.

SOCRATES: And we divided the divine kind of madness into

four parts, each with its own deity. We attributed prophetic inspiration to Apollo, mystical inspiration to Dionysus, poetic inspiration to the Muses, and the fourth kind to Aphrodite and to Love. We said that the madness of love was the best kind, and we came up with some sort of analogy for it. We may have touched on the truth to a certain extent, or we may also have been led astray; but anyway we cobbled together a not entirely implausible speech, and in an appropriate and respectful manner we sang a light-hearted c hymn, in the form of a story, in honour of your master and mine, Phaedrus—Love, the god responsible for beautiful boys.

PHAEDRUS: And I really enjoyed listening to it.

SOCRATES: Well, the aspect of it I'd like us to focus on is how the speech managed to change from criticism to praise.*

PHAEDRUS: What exactly do you mean?

SOCRATES: It seems to me that although in actual fact the speech was basically playful, still there were two features whose significance—since they did fortuitously crop up in the speech—it would not be unrewarding to grasp in a d skilful manner.

PHAEDRUS: What are these features?

SOCRATES: First, bringing things which are scattered all over the place into a single class by gaining a comprehensive view of them, so that one can define any given thing and so clarify the topic one wants to explain at any time.* That's what we did just now, when we were trying to explain what love is by defining it first: whether or not we were right, our speech did at least achieve clarity and internal consistency thanks to this procedure.

PHAEDRUS: And what was the other feature you meant, Socrates?

SOCRATES: Being able to cut things up again, class by class, e according to their natural joints, rather than trying to break them up as an incompetent butcher might.* Just as, not long ago, my two speeches took the irrational part of the mind as

55

a single type of thing, with features in common, and just as a
single body has parts that naturally come in pairs with the
266a same names (one called the part on the left and the other the
part on the right), so my two speeches regarded insanity as a
single natural type of thing in us, and one speech cut off the
part to the left, and then went on cutting this part up until it
had discovered among the sections a kind of love which one
might call 'on the left hand'* (and which it abused as it fully
deserves), while the other speech led us to the right-hand
types of madness and discovered a section which may have
the same name as the other, but is divine (and which it
praised, once it had displayed it to our view, as responsible
b for all the most important benefits that come our way).*

PHAEDRUS: You're perfectly right.

SOCRATES: Now I am enamoured of these divisions and collections, Phaedrus, because I want to be good at speaking
and thinking, and if I think anyone else is capable of discerning a natural unity and plurality, I follow 'hard on his heels,
as if he were a god'.* Moreover, I call those who are capable
of doing this—only the gods know whether or not this is the
right term, but so far I've been calling them 'dialecticians'.*
c But tell me what I should call them now that we've been
taught by you and Lysias. Or is the correct term just what
we've been talking about, expertise at speaking, which
Thrasymachus and so on use to become skilful speakers
themselves, and which they also impart to anyone else who
is prepared to bring them gifts, as if they were royalty?*

PHAEDRUS: Well, they may act like royalty, but they certainly
don't have the knowledge you're asking about. No, I think
your term 'dialectic' is correct for this kind of ability, but it
seems to me that we haven't yet pinned rhetoric down.

d SOCRATES: What do you mean? Is there possibly something
worthwhile which is liable to expertise, but in which collection and division are not involved? If so, you and I must do
all we can not to belittle it. We must state exactly what the
remaining part of rhetoric is.

PHAEDRUS: There are plenty of aspects left, of course, Socrates—those that have been written down in the handbooks on rhetoric.

SOCRATES: Yes, I'm glad you reminded me of them. First of all, I think there's the instruction to start the speech with a 'preamble'. These are the rhetorical refinements you meant, aren't they?

PHAEDRUS: Yes.   e

SOCRATES: Second, there's the 'exposition', as I think it is called, followed by the 'evidence of witnesses'. Third, there are 'proofs', and fourth, 'arguments from probability'.* And I think that wonderful Byzantine word-wizard, at any rate, talks next of 'confirmation' and 'extra confirmation'.

PHAEDRUS: You mean the good Theodorus.

SOCRATES: Of course. Oh yes, he also recommends 'refuta- 267a tion' and 'extra refutation', whether one is prosecuting or defending. And how can we fail to bring forward the excellent Evenus of Paros, who was the first to invent 'insinuation' and 'indirect praise'?† It's also said that his speeches included indirect censures written in verse to make them memorable. He's a clever fellow. And shall we leave Tisias and Gorgias asleep, when they saw that arguments from probability were preferable to the truth? They also used the power of speech to make trivia appear important and important things trivial, they got novelties to sound old and old things fresh and new, and whatever the subject they b discovered how to pare their speech right down or extend it indefinitely. Prodicus once heard me saying this and he replied with a laugh that he alone had discovered the professional way of speaking: speeches should not be long or short, he said, but just the right length.

PHAEDRUS: Very clever, Prodicus!

SOCRATES: We'd better mention Hippias, because I think our visitor from Elis would agree with Prodicus.

PHAEDRUS: Of course he would.

SOCRATES: And what shall we say next about Polus' gallery of

learned terms such as 'reduplication', 'quotation of
c maxims', and 'use of images', and about the dictionary
Licymnius gave him to help him make the correct use of
language?

PHAEDRUS: Didn't Protagoras do similar work, actually?

SOCRATES: Yes, my young friend, he did a lot of fine work,
especially on 'correct diction', as I think it is called. Then
there's the technique, which I think the mighty Chalcedonian* has skilfully mastered, of dragging on speeches
designed to arouse pity for old age and poverty. The man
has also developed the skill of making a whole crowd of
d people angry, and then calming their anger with incanta-
tions, as he puts it. And there's no one better than him at
both character assassination and the refutation of character assassination from any source. As for the conclusion
of speeches, everyone seems to be in agreement, though
some call it the 'recapitulation' and others use other
names.

PHAEDRUS: You mean summarizing points as a means of
reminding the audience at the end of what has been said?

SOCRATES: Yes—but do you have anything to add on the
subject of rhetorical expertise?

PHAEDRUS: Nothing important—nothing worth mentioning.

268a SOCRATES: Well, let's not bother with the unimportant points.
But let's have a closer look, in good light, at what we've
already said, to see just what† skilful rhetoric can achieve.

PHAEDRUS: It's extremely influential in mass meetings, Socrates, at any rate.

SOCRATES: Yes, it is. But I'd like you to look and see, my
friend, if you agree with me that there are holes in the fabric
of the points we've already raised.

PHAEDRUS: Do please show me where these holes are.

SOCRATES: Well, here's a question for you. Suppose someone
came up to your friend Eryximachus or his father Acumenus, and said, 'I know how to treat the body in ways
b which allow me to raise or lower temperatures, to get people

to vomit, to make their bowels move, and so on and so forth
—whatever I choose or decide is best. And since I have this
knowledge I regard myself as a professional doctor, and I
claim to be able to make others doctors too by imparting this
knowledge to them.' How do you think they would respond
to this speech?

PHAEDRUS: I'm sure they'd ask him whether he also knew
whom he should treat in these ways, and when, and how
much.

SOCRATES: And what if he said, 'No, I don't. But I claim that
anyone who learnt these treatments from me would be able
to do what you ask'?   c

PHAEDRUS: I think they'd say that the man was out of his
mind, and was imagining that he'd become a doctor after
having heard someone reading from some book or other, or
after having accidentally come across some minor drugs, but
that he really had no understanding of this area of expertise.

SOCRATES: And what if someone went up to Sophocles or
Euripides and claimed to know how to compose huge, long
speeches on trivial topics and very short ones on important
topics, and said that he could choose to make the speeches
sad or, alternatively, frightening and threatening and so on?
And suppose he went on to say that he fancied himself a
teacher of the art of composing tragedies because he could   d
teach others how to do these things.

PHAEDRUS: I think they'd laugh at him as well, Socrates, for
imagining that a tragedy is anything other than the
arrangement of these speeches in such a way that they fit in
with one another and conform to the whole.

SOCRATES: But I don't suppose they'd be coarse or rude to
him. Suppose a musician met a man who fancied himself an
expert on harmony because he happened to know how to
produce the highest and lowest notes on a lyre. The musician wouldn't bluntly retort, 'You poor, deluded fool!' No,   e
as a musician he'd say something more gentle: 'My dear
fellow, although it's true that the knowledge you have is vital

for musicianship, it's perfectly possible for someone in your position to know absolutely nothing about harmony. What you know are the essential prerequisites to music, but not music itself.'*

PHAEDRUS: You're quite right.

269a SOCRATES: And the same goes for Sophocles too. He'd tell the person who was showing off to him and Euripides that he knew the preliminaries to tragedy, but not the actual art of tragedy, and Acumenus would tell his man that he knew the preliminaries to medicine, but not the actual art of medicine.

PHAEDRUS: Absolutely.

SOCRATES: And what do we think would happen if 'honey-tongued Adrastus'* or Pericles were to hear of any of the wonderful techniques we were just discussing—'concision' and 'use of images' and all the other techniques we went through and said we should look at in good light? Would

b   they lay into him, as you and I would? Would they be so rude as to say something coarse to the people who have written books on these techniques and teach them as if they constituted rhetorical expertise? Or, since they're cleverer than us, would they tell us off too and say: 'Phaedrus and Socrates, rather than getting cross you should feel sorry for people who prove incapable of defining rhetoric because they are ignorant of dialectic. As a result of this ignorance they thought they had discovered what rhetoric was when they had learnt only the necessary prerequisites to rhetorical

c   expertise. They think that if they teach others these pre-liminaries they've taught all there is to rhetoric, and that their pupils should draw on their own resources to equip their speeches with irrelevancies like how to put these techniques to persuasive use, and how to put together a whole, rounded speech.'

PHAEDRUS: Well, Socrates, it does look as though the area of expertise which these men teach and write about as rhetoric is pretty much as you've described. I think you're right. But where does the expertise of a true orator, a persuasive speaker, come from? How could one get it?   d

SOCRATES: It seems likely, Phaedrus, and perhaps it's even inevitable, that the ability to become a perfect performer in this sphere depends on the same factors as it does in every other sphere. If you naturally have what it takes to be an expert orator, you'll be a famous orator, once you have supplemented natural ability with knowledge and practice. If you lack any of these three factors, you'll be less than perfect in that respect. But in so far as there's a technical aspect to rhetoric, I'm not convinced that the way Lysias and Thrasymachus go about it is right.

PHAEDRUS: How should they go about it, then?

SOCRATES: The fact that there was no one who could beat e Pericles as an accomplished orator is really pretty much what you'd expect, my friend.*

PHAEDRUS: Why?

SOCRATES: Every area of expertise of any importance requires one to be a windbag natural scientist with one's head in the clouds,* since that seems to be where loftiness of perspective 270a and all-round effectiveness come from. And Pericles did supplement his natural ability like this. As a result of falling in with Anaxagoras, who was just that sort of person, I think, he became infected with this lofty perspective, reached an understanding of the nature of mind and mindlessness† (which Anaxagoras famously used to discuss a lot), and applied to his rhetorical expertise whatever he gained from this source that was appropriate.

PHAEDRUS: What do you mean?

SOCRATES: I think you could say that medicine and rhetoric b use the same method.

PHAEDRUS: In what sense?

SOCRATES: In both cases you have to determine the nature of something—the body in medicine and the soul in rhetoric— if you're going to be an expert practitioner, rather than relying merely on an experiential knack. In the one case you employ drugs and diet to give the body health and strength, and in the other case you employ speeches to give the soul whatever convictions you want, and lawful practices to make it virtuous.

PHAEDRUS: Yes, that seems plausible, Socrates.

c SOCRATES: Well, do you think one could understand the nature of soul satisfactorily without knowledge of the nature of the whole?*

PHAEDRUS: If Hippocrates the Asclepiad is right, one can't understand the body properly either without going about it in this way.

SOCRATES: Yes, and he's right, my friend. But as well as Hippocrates, we must examine the argument to see if it makes sense.

PHAEDRUS: I agree.

SOCRATES: So have a look and see what both Hippocrates and the true argument are saying about the nature of things. When considering the nature of anything at all, shouldn't

d we first see whether what we want to become experts in, and to make others experts in, is simple or complex? Next, if it's simple, shouldn't we try to see what natural capacity it has for acting and on what it acts, or what natural capacity it has for being acted upon and by what it is acted upon? And if it's complex, shouldn't we enumerate all its aspects and do the same with each of these aspects as we did with the simple thing—that is, see with which of these aspects it is naturally equipped to act and to what effect, or with which of these aspects it is naturally equipped to be acted upon, by what, and to what effect?

PHAEDRUS: I suppose so, Socrates.

SOCRATES: At any rate, proceeding without having taken these steps is like a blind man making a journey. But the

e analogy with blindness or deafness must fail when someone goes about his subject skilfully. No, it's obvious that if someone sets about skilfully teaching another person rhetoric, he will demonstrate with precision the essential nature of that towards which his pupil is to direct his speeches—which is, as you know, the soul.

PHAEDRUS: Of course.

SOCRATES: So the soul is what he focuses all his efforts on, 271a since it is the soul in which he is trying to produce conviction. Right?

PHAEDRUS: Yes.

SOCRATES: It obviously follows that Thrasymachus and anyone else who takes the teaching of rhetorical expertise seriously will first describe the soul with such absolute precision that we are able to see whether it has a single, uniform nature, or whether it is complex, like the body. For this is what we're saying it is to reveal the nature of anything.

PHAEDRUS: Absolutely.

SOCRATES: Second, he will show with which of its aspects it is naturally equipped to act or be acted upon, and in either case to what effect.

PHAEDRUS: Of course.

SOCRATES: Third, once he has classified the types of speech b and of soul, and the ways in which the various types of soul are acted upon, he will go through all the causes, fitting each type of speech to each type of soul and explaining what it is about the nature of particular kinds of soul which makes them inevitably either persuaded or unpersuaded by speeches of a particular kind.

PHAEDRUS: Yes, it looks as though that would be best.

SOCRATES: In fact, my friend, whatever the subject of a speech—whether it's what we've been talking about or anything else, and whether the speech is a model or actually delivered—it's only by following this procedure that it will be professionally spoken or written about. But the people c you've heard, our current writers of rhetorical manuals, are scoundrels who disguise the fact that they are perfectly knowledgeable about soul. So until they adhere to the following procedure in their speeches and written works, let's not believe that they are experts at speech-writing.

PHAEDRUS: What procedure?

SOCRATES: It's not easy to give the actual words,* but I'm prepared to say how to write speeches with the maximum possible expertise.

PHAEDRUS: Go on.

SOCRATES: Since it's the function of speech to lead the soul, a
d would-be orator must know how many types of soul there are. So, 'There are so many types of soul, with such-and-such qualities, which is why some people are like this and others are like that.' After dividing souls up in this way, 'There are so many types of speech, each of such-and-such a kind. People with such-and-such a nature are easy to persuade of such-and-such by speeches of such-and-such a type for reason x, while people with such-and-such a nature are hard to persuade for reason y.' Once our would-be orator has a good intellectual understanding of all this, he should next observe souls actually involved in and being
e affected by events, using his senses to pay keen attention to them, or else he won't yet be gaining anything from the discussions he heard at school. When he can not only say what kind of person is persuaded by what kind of speech, but also spot that kind of person before him and tell himself that here, in real life and before his eyes, is the kind of
272a person and the kind of character which was the subject of those earlier discussions, and to which such-and-such a kind of speech should be applied in such-and-such a way to persuade him of such-and-such—once he is capable of doing all this, and moreover has understood the proper moments for speaking and for keeping quiet, and can also recognize the appropriate and inappropriate occasions for concision, arousing pity, shocking the audience, and all the various modes of speech he has learnt, then and only then will his expertise have been perfected and completed. But if in his speaking or teaching or writing a person falls short
b in any of these respects, but still claims to be an expert speaker, the correct response is disbelief. 'Well, Phaedrus

and Socrates,' our writer might ask, 'do you agree, or†
should we accept some alternative description of rhetorical
expertise?'

PHAEDRUS: We can't accept any alternative, Socrates, but
expertise does seem to be quite an arduous business.

SOCRATES: You're right, and that's exactly why we must turn
all our arguments upside down to see if we can somehow
find an easier and shorter route to it, so that no one need go c
pointlessly off on a long, rough road when he could take a
short, smooth one. If you can offer any help—you might
have heard something from Lysias or someone else—do
please try to remember it and tell me.

PHAEDRUS: I would if trying was all that was needed, but as
things are I can't, not just like that.

SOCRATES: So shall I tell you an argument I've heard from
some of the professionals in this area?

PHAEDRUS: By all means.

SOCRATES: Yes, Phaedrus, because it's only fair to present the
wolf's tale too, as the saying goes.*

PHAEDRUS: Then please do just that.   d

SOCRATES: Well, according to these people there's no need for
such a bombastic approach to the subject, nor for taking the
long and circuitous route involved in referring things back
to first principles, because—as in fact we said at the beginning of this discussion*—there's absolutely no need for a
person planning to be a competent orator to have anything
to do with the truth where right or good actions are concerned, or indeed where right or good people are concerned, whether they are so by nature or nurture. They say
that in the lawcourts no one has the slightest interest in the
truth of these things, but only in making a plausible case;
and since it is probability that enables one to do that, then e
this is what someone who plans to be an expert orator
should concentrate on. In fact sometimes, they say, you
shouldn't even mention what actually happened, if it is
improbable, but make up a plausible tale instead, when

prosecuting and when defending. Whatever kind of speech one is giving, one should aim for probability (which often means saying farewell to the truth), because rhetorical skill depends entirely on one's speeches being infused throughout by probability.

273a

PHAEDRUS: Socrates, that's a perfect account of what the self-professed rhetorical experts say. I mean, I remembered that we touched briefly on something like this before, but it seems to be the absolute crux of the matter for the professionals.

SOCRATES: But you've thoroughly studied Tisias' own words, at least, so let's have Tisias also tell us whether by 'what is probable' he means anything other than 'what the masses suppose to be the case'.

b

PHAEDRUS: No, that's exactly it.

SOCRATES: It was presumably after making this clever and professional discovery that he explained in his book what should happen if someone who is weak and brave beats up a strong coward, steals his coat or something, and is taken to court. Neither of them should tell the truth. The coward should deny that he was beaten up by just the one man, the brave one, who in turn should contend that they were alone, and then deploy the famous argument: 'How could someone like me have attacked someone like him?' The coward will of course not mention his own cowardice, but will try to come up with some other lie, which may give his opponent an opportunity to challenge him. And in every situation professional arguments will look something like that, won't they, Phaedrus?

c

PHAEDRUS: Of course.

SOCRATES: Well, it certainly looks as though it was a wonderfully recondite profession that Tisias discovered—or whoever else it might have been, whatever he likes to be called after.* Still, my friend, are we or are we not to tell him . . .

d PHAEDRUS: What?

SOCRATES: 'In actual fact, Tisias, we've been saying for a long

66

time, since before you came along, that this probability of yours actually takes root in the minds of the masses because of its similarity to the truth, and not long ago* we concluded that in every sphere it is those who know the truth who are best able to come up with similarities. So we'll listen to you if you have anything else to say about rhetorical expertise, but if you don't we'll trust our recent conclusions. We said that unless a person had enumerated the characters of the members of his audience, and unless he could divide things e class by class and take every individual thing, one by one, and see how it falls within a single category, he would never achieve rhetorical expertise to the extent that a human being can. But there's no way that he will ever gain these abilities without a great deal of effort. Now, a sensible person should not expend all that effort in order to speak and act in the world of men, but in order to be able to make speeches that are pleasing to the gods and to act, whatever he is doing, in ways that gratify them, to the limits of his abilities. For as I'm sure you're aware, Tisias, those of us with more than the usual wisdom say that anyone with any sense should not cultivate the gratification of his fellow slaves, except incidentally, but that of his masters, who are thoroughly good. 274a So you shouldn't be surprised if the route is long and circuitous, because the goals for which the journey is undertaken are important, not the trivial ones you suppose.* Nevertheless, our argument claims that these trivial goals too will best come about as a result of a person's being prepared to pursue the important ones.'

PHAEDRUS: I think your argument is truly excellent, Socrates —if only one could put it into practice!

SOCRATES: But if someone even attempts something fine, whatever happens to him is fine too. b

PHAEDRUS: All right.

SOCRATES: Is this enough on the subject of rhetorical expertise and its lack?

PHAEDRUS: Of course.

SOCRATES: But don't we still have to discuss whether or not writing is desirable—what makes it acceptable and what makes it undesirable?*

PHAEDRUS: Yes.

SOCRATES: So do you know the best way for either a theoretical or a practical approach to speech to please god?

PHAEDRUS: No, I don't. Do you?

c SOCRATES: Well, I can pass on something I've heard from our predecessors. Only they know the truth of the matter, but if we had made this discovery by ourselves, would we any longer have the slightest interest in mere human conjectures?

PHAEDRUS: What an absurd question! Please tell me what you say you've heard.

SOCRATES: All right. The story I heard* is set in Naucratis in Egypt, where there was one of the ancient gods of Egypt— the one to whom the bird they call the 'ibis' is sacred, whose name is Theuth. This deity was the inventor of number, d arithmetic, geometry, and astronomy, of games involving draughts and dice—and especially of writing. At the time, the king of the whole of Egypt around the capital city of the inland region (the city the Greeks call 'Egyptian Thebes'*), was Thamous, or Amon, as the Greeks call him.† Theuth came to Thamous and showed him the branches of expertise he had invented, and suggested that they should be spread throughout Egypt. Thamous asked him what good each one would do, and subjected Theuth's explanations to e criticism if he thought he was going wrong and praise if thought he was right. The story goes that Thamous expressed himself at length to Theuth about each of the branches of expertise, both for and against them. It would take a long time to go through all Thamous' views, but when it was the turn of writing, Theuth said, 'Your highness, this science will increase the intelligence of the people of Egypt and improve their memories. For this invention is a potion for memory and intelligence.' But Thamous replied, 'You are most ingenious, Theuth. But one person has the ability to bring branches of expertise into existence, another to assess the extent to which they will harm or benefit those who use them. The loyalty you feel to writing, as its originator, has just led you to tell me the opposite of its true effect. 275a It will atrophy people's memories.* Trust in writing will make them remember things by relying on marks made by others, from outside themselves, not on their own inner resources,* and so writing will make the things they have learnt disappear from their minds. Your invention is a potion for jogging the memory, not for remembering. You provide your students with the appearance of intelligence, not real intelligence. Because your students will be widely read, though without any contact with a teacher, they will seem to be men of wide knowledge, when they will usually b be ignorant. And this spurious appearance of intelligence will make them difficult company.'

PHAEDRUS: Socrates, it doesn't take much for you to make up stories from Egypt and anywhere else in the world you feel like.

SOCRATES: Well, my friend, the people at the sanctuary of Zeus at Dodona say that the original prophecies there were spoken by an oak.* In those days people weren't as clever as you young ones nowadays, and they were so foolish that they happily listened to oak and rock,* as long as they told the truth. But perhaps it matters to you who the speaker is, c or what country he's from, because you are not concerned only with whether or not he is right.

PHAEDRUS: You're right to have told me off—and, yes, I think the Theban king was correct about writing.

SOCRATES: So anyone who thinks he can get a branch of expertise to survive by committing it to writing—and also anyone who inherits the work with the assumption that writing will give him something clear and reliable—would be behaving in a thoroughly foolish manner and really would be ignorant of Amon's prediction, if he supposed

that written words could do more than jog the memory of
d   someone who already knows the topic that has been written
about.

PHAEDRUS: Quite so.

SOCRATES: Yes, because there's something odd about writing,
Phaedrus, which makes it exactly like painting. The offspring of painting stand there as if alive, but if you ask them
a question they maintain an aloof silence.* It's the same with
written words: you might think they were speaking as if they
had some intelligence, but if you want an explanation of any
of the things they're saying and you ask them about it, they
just go on and on for ever giving the same single piece of
information. Once any account has been written down, you
e   find it all over the place, hobnobbing with completely
inappropriate people no less than with those who understand it, and completely failing to know who it should and
shouldn't talk to. And faced with rudeness and unfair abuse
it always needs its father to come to its assistance, since it is
incapable of defending or helping itself.*

PHAEDRUS: Again, you're quite right.

276a   SOCRATES: Well, is there any other way of using words? Does
the written word have a legitimate brother? Can we see how
it is born, and how much better and stronger it grows than
its brother?

PHAEDRUS: What is this way of using words? How is it born,
do you think?

SOCRATES: It is the kind that is written along with knowledge
in the soul of a student. It is capable of defending itself, and
it knows how to speak to those it should and keep silent in
the company of those to whom it shouldn't speak.

PHAEDRUS: You're talking about the living, ensouled speech
of a man of knowledge. We'd be right to describe the written
word as a mere image of this.*

b   SOCRATES: Absolutely. So here's another question for you.
Consider a sensible farmer who cares for his seeds and
wants to see them come to fruition. Do you think he'd

happily spend time and effort planting them in the summer in gardens of Adonis,* and watch them grow up in eight days, or would he do this, if at all, as a diversion and for the sake of a festival? Don't you think that for seeds he was serious about he'd draw on his skill as a farmer, sow them in the appropriate soil, and be content if what he sowed reached maturity in the eighth month?

PHAEDRUS: Yes, that's what he'd do, Socrates. He'd take care c of the one lot of seeds and treat the others differently, just as you said.

SOCRATES: So are we to say that someone who knows about right and fine and good activities* is less sensible than our farmer where his own seeds are concerned?

PHAEDRUS: Of course not.

SOCRATES: Then he won't spend time and effort writing what he knows in water—in black water*—and sowing them with his pen by means of words which can neither speak in their own defence nor come up with a satisfactory explanation of the truth.

PHAEDRUS: No, it's hardly likely that he will.

SOCRATES: No. He'll probably sow and write his gardens d of letters for amusement, if at all, as a way of storing up things to jog his own memory when 'he reaches the age of forgetfulness',* and also the memory of anyone else who is pursuing the same course as him. He'll happily watch these delicate gardens growing, and he'll presumably spend his time diverting himself with them rather than the symposia and so on with which other people amuse themselves.

PHAEDRUS: What a wonderful kind of diversion you're e describing, Socrates—that of a person who can amuse himself with words, as he tells stories about justice and the other things you mentioned—compared with the trivial pastimes of others!

SOCRATES: Yes, that's right, my dear Phaedrus. But it's far better, in my opinion, to treat justice and so on seriously, which is what happens when an expert dialectician takes hold of a suitable soul and uses his knowledge to plant and sow the kinds of words which are capable of defending both themselves and the one who planted them. So far from being barren, these words bear a seed from which other words grow in other environments. This makes them capable of giving everlasting life to the original seed, and of making the man who has them as happy as it is possible for a mortal man to be.

PHAEDRUS: Yes, this is certainly far better.

SOCRATES: With this conclusion in place, Phaedrus, we are at last in a position to reach a verdict about the other issue.

PHAEDRUS: What other issue?

SOCRATES: The one that brought us here. We wanted to investigate why Lysias was abused for writing speeches, and the expert or inexpert composition of the actual speeches. Well, I think we've made it fairly clear what makes for expertise and its lack.

PHAEDRUS: I thought so, but could you remind me again?

SOCRATES: First, someone has to know the truth of every matter he's speaking or writing about, which is to say that he has to be capable of defining a whole as it is in itself and then know how to divide it up class by class until he reaches something indivisible. He also has to be able to distinguish souls in the same sort of way, discover the kind of speech which naturally fits each kind of soul, and organize and arrange his speeches accordingly—offering a complex soul a complex speech which covers the whole range of modes, and a simple soul a simple speech.* Until he can do all this he will be incapable of tackling speeches in as much of a professional manner as their nature allows, either for teaching or for persuasion. This is what the whole of our earlier discussion has shown us.

PHAEDRUS: Yes, absolutely. That's pretty much what we found.

SOCRATES: So what about the question whether or not it is acceptable to deliver or write speeches, and under what circumstances it would or would not be fair to describe it as a shameful activity? Haven't our recent conclusions shown . . .

PHAEDRUS: What conclusions?

SOCRATES: . . . that if Lysias or anyone else who has in the past written a speech, or will write one in the future, for private or public consumption—that is, in the latter case, when proposing legislation and so composing a political speech—thinks there is any great degree of reliability and clarity in it, this is a source of shame for the author, whether or not anyone has ever said as much to him. For, awake or asleep, ignorance about what activities are right and wrong and good and bad cannot, when seen aright, fail to be a matter for reproach, even if the general mass of people approve of it.   e

PHAEDRUS: I quite agree.

SOCRATES: But consider someone who thinks that, whatever the subject, a written speech is bound to be largely a source of amusement, and that no speech which has ever been written in verse or in prose deserves to be taken seriously; that the same goes for the declamations of rhapsodes,* which are designed to produce conviction, but allow no cross-examination and contain no element of teaching; that in actual fact the best speeches do no more than jog the memories of men of knowledge; that clarity and perfection and something worth taking seriously are to be found only in words which are used for explanation and teaching, and are truly written in the soul, on the subject of right and fine and good activities; that, while he ignores all the rest, words of this kind should be attributed to him as his legitimate sons— above all the words within himself, if he has found them and they are there, but secondly the words that are at once the offspring and the brothers of these internal ones of his, and have duly grown in others' souls. It looks, Phaedrus, as though anyone with these views has attained the condition you and I can only pray for.   278a

   b

PHAEDRUS: I have no hesitation at all in wishing and praying for what you've said.

SOCRATES: So now we've diverted ourselves for long enough on the subject of speeches. It's up to you to go and tell Lysias of our excursion to the Nymphs' spring and the Muses' shrine. Explain to him how we listened to speeches

c which commanded us to tell Lysias (and any other composer of speeches), Homer (and any other author of poetry, whether accompanied or unaccompanied by music), and thirdly Solon (and anyone else who writes legislation, as he calls it—which is to say, written compositions in the form of political speeches) that if he has written from a position of knowledge of how things truly are, if he can mount a defence when challenged on the content of his work, and if he can produce arguments of his own to prove the unimportance of what he has written, then he does not deserve a title derived from these pursuits,* but a description

d based on the things he takes seriously.

PHAEDRUS: What names are you thinking of giving him?

SOCRATES: I think it's too much to call him 'wise', Phaedrus: only the gods deserve that label. But it would suit him better and be more appropriate to call him a lover of wisdom,* or something like that.

PHAEDRUS: Yes, that would fit the bill.

SOCRATES: On the other hand, wouldn't you be right to use the titles 'poet' or 'speech-writer' or 'law-writer' for someone who has nothing more valuable than the composition or piece of writing he has arrived at by a lengthy process of

e turning upside down, and by cutting and pasting the various parts into different relations with one another?

PHAEDRUS: Of course.

SOCRATES: Then this is what you should tell your friend.

PHAEDRUS: And what about you? What are you going to do? After all, we surely shouldn't ignore your friend as well.

SOCRATES: Who's that?

PHAEDRUS: The beautiful Isocrates.* What are you going to tell him, Socrates? What shall we call him?

SOCRATES: Isocrates is still young, Phaedrus, but I'd like to tell you what I guess the future holds for him.   279a

PHAEDRUS: What?

SOCRATES: He strikes me as being naturally more talented than Lysias and his crowd,† and also to have a nobler temperament. So it wouldn't surprise me at all if, as he matured, he came to stand out among everyone else who has ever undertaken speech-writing, as an adult among children and more so—and that's considering the kinds of speeches he is currently engaged on. I think he'd stand out even more if he wasn't content with his present work, and some more divine impulse were to guide him towards greater things. For he does innately have a certain philosophical cast to his mind, my friend. So that's the message I shall bring b Isocrates, as my beloved, from the gods of this place, and you already know what to tell your beloved Lysias.

PHAEDRUS: All right. But let's go, now that the weather has cooled down.

SOCRATES: Shouldn't one first pray to the gods here before setting off?

PHAEDRUS: Of course.

SOCRATES: Dear Pan and all gods here, grant that I may become beautiful within and that my external possessions may be congruent with my inner state. May I take wisdom c for wealth, and may I have just as much gold as a moderate person, and no one else, could bear and carry by himself. Have I missed anything out, Phaedrus? This prayer will do for me.*

PHAEDRUS: Say the prayer for me too. For friends share everything.*

SOCRATES: Let's go.

EXPLANATORY NOTES

See also the Index of Names (pp. 107–11) for information on characters appearing or mentioned in the dialogue.

227a *the city walls*: the dramatic date of this dialogue cannot be fixed, largely because there are too many uncertainties in the lives of the people involved. Lysias was (probably) not resident in Athens until after 412, and his brother Polemarchus, who died in 404, is presumed still to be alive (257b). During this period, however, Phaedrus was in exile. We might be tempted to suppose that Lysias paid a visit to Athens from his home in southern Italy some time earlier, perhaps during the lull in the Peloponnesian War around 420, but by this time, although he had undoubtedly studied rhetoric, he had not embarked on a career as a speech-writer. K. J. Dover (*Lysias and the Corpus Lysiacum* (Berkeley: University of California Press, 1968), 32–4), supposing that Lysias was already resident in Athens, argues for a date early in 415, before Phaedrus went into exile, but it seems unlikely that Lysias was well known as a speech-writer by then either. It seems that, as elsewhere, Plato is being anachronistic or careless about the dramatic date of the dialogue. At any rate, throughout this period, Athens had impressive defensive walls, which not only sur-rounded the city, but also connected it to the port of Piraeus (these connecting walls were demolished after Athens' defeat in 404). It is outside the main city walls, to the south-east of the city (see the first note on 229a), that we may picture Socrates and Phaedrus taking their walk, having left through the Itonia Gate. For more precise details, see R. E. Wycherley, 'The Scene of Plato's *Phaidros*', *Phoenix*, 17 (1963), 88–98.

The date of composition of the dialogue is just as difficult to fix. Most scholars regard it as one of Plato's later, or late-middle-period works, composed around 370 BCE. On the shaky grounds that Lysias was still alive until about 366, and that Plato would not have been so rude to a living person, Panagiotou argues for a later date, during or just after 365 (S. Panagiotou, 'Lysias and the Date of Plato's *Phaedrus*', *Mnemosyne*, 28 (1975), 388–98). For various views, see the essays in the section 'Relative Chronology' in Rossetti [19].

227a *ever since daybreak*: this was the normal time for activities to start, so that they would be over by the time the weather got too hot. We may imagine the dialogue starting late in the morning, towards noon (229a).

227b *in the porticoes*: the covered colonnades or stoas of Athens, used for socializing, strolling, and some sports. Modern visitors to Athens have the benefit of a reconstructed Stoa of Attalus in the agora.

227b *Lysias is in town, apparently*: as a 'metic', a foreign resident of Athens, for all his wealth Lysias was not allowed to own property in Athens itself. He lived, along with most other metics, in Piraeus, the port and commercial centre of Athens.

227b *temple of Olympian Zeus*: to the east of the Acropolis. The temple appears to have been incomplete at the time, and remained so for centuries. The tall columns which can still be seen in Athens date from the time of the Roman emperor Hadrian (second century CE).

227b *feast of words*: according to Rowe [3], a slightly mocking tone characterizes this prologue. Socrates will not only gently mock Phaedrus for this devotion to Lysias, but is perhaps sarcastic in his praise of their final stopping-place (230b–c). Just as Socrates is out of the city—his normal haunt (230d)—so Plato is making him aloof from Phaedrus and his concerns. We are prepared to find, later in the dialogue, that rhetoric is not entirely to be taken seriously—or at any rate that content is more important than the form to which Phaedrus is devoted.

227b *to quote Pindar*: the phrase is taken from Pindar's first Isthmian poem, line 2. As well as the explicit quotations which occur from time to time in *Phaedrus* (and which I have noted), scholars have found more remote echoes from poets such as Pindar and Euripides in the dialogue. These echoes are not implausible in a work of such literary polish.

227c *about love*: Socrates is a suitable audience for such a speech because he claimed ignorance about almost everything except 'the ways of love' (*Symposium* 177d, 198d, imitated by the author of the pseudo-Platonic *Theages* at 128b). In addition to the philosophical aspect of love developed in *Phaedrus* and *Symposium*, Socrates was also physically attracted to several of his young companions: see, for instance, the opening scene of Plato's *Charmides*.

227d *as Herodicus recommends*: Megara is a town about 26 miles (42 kilometres) to the west of Athens—and so in exactly the opposite direction from that which Socrates and Phaedrus are taking. Its mention is triggered by the thought of Herodicus, who came from there, and seems to have recommended some form of exercise involving walking up to the walls and back again, perhaps from a fixed point such as the town centre, so as to guarantee walking a certain distance a day.

228b *by the dog*: a euphemistic oath peculiar but not exclusive to Socrates. *Gorgias* 482b suggests that it may have originated as an oath by the dog-headed Egyptian god Anubis, the psychopomp of the dead. If so, since *Phaedrus* is about leading souls (in an educational sense), the oath is peculiarly appropriate here.

228b *sick with passion for hearing speeches*: the first hint of the metaphor linking sickness and passion which will become important in the dialogue.

228c *an unwilling audience*: this speech is 'a minor parody of the techniques attributed later in the dialogue to the rhetorician Tisias' (Rowe [3], 137), in that it builds up a case based entirely on plausibility.

228e *show me what you've got*: the erotic overtones of Socrates' wanting to see inside Phaedrus' cloak are deliberate (see J. Partridge, 'Socratic Dialectic and the Art of Love: *Phaedrus* 276e–277a', in K. A. Rosenbecker and J. L. Adamitis (eds), *Representations of Philosophy in the Classical World* (*Ancient Philosophy*, 19 (1999), special issue), 121–32); similarly, at *Charmides* 155d, a glimpse inside Charmides' cloak is enough to arouse him. In our dialogue, Socrates has been behaving like a lover—a lover of speeches (228b–c), even if not quite a lover of Phaedrus—and declares himself ready to follow Phaedrus all over the place (230d–e), like a besotted lover.

228e *producing the written speech*: this 'stage direction' is not in the Greek. This is an odd bit of byplay between Socrates and Phaedrus, and seems intended to be significant. Perhaps it is a parody of the lover's approach to Beauty as outlined in Socrates' great speech (and in *Symposium*): Socrates is first offered a taste in the form of remembered extracts (note how memory later in the dialogue is our means of access to images of Beauty etc. in this world), but finally the real thing. Phaedrus' concern with images is underlined at 235d–e and 236b.

229a *the Ilissus*: Athens was bracketed, so to speak, by two rivers: the Eridanus which flowed from east of the city, past the agora, and out to the west, and the Ilissus to the south-east of the city, outside the walls. In what follows, the reader's attention is drawn to Socrates' and Phaedrus' surroundings more, and more pointedly, than in any other Platonic dialogue. But few will want to go as far as Ferrari, who interprets this as 'an example and emblem of interaction between "foreground" and "background" of competence: between that aspect which is or can be made explicit, and that which is either contextually or, it may be, essentially tacit' ([16], pp. 30–1).

229a *You never do, of course*: Socrates' habit of going without footwear was famous enough to feature in the sketch of him drawn by Aristophanes in *Clouds* (423 BCE), and is mentioned several times by Plato and Xenophon too. His asceticism is portrayed most famously by Plato at *Symposium* 220b. But it was asceticism, rather than poverty. While there is no doubt that Socrates neglected money-making in favour of philosophizing, he was not born poor: he served as a hoplite in the Athenian army, which is a sign of the relatively well-to-do middle class.

229c *two or three stades*: a stade was 600 Greek feet—about 195 yards or 177 metres.

229c *Agra*: one of the Attic demes or villages lying outside Athens.

229c *by Zeus*: to swear by Zeus in this kind of context just adds emphasis. The sentence might have been translated as: 'But tell me, Socrates, please.' But given the number of oaths in this part of *Phaedrus*, and the mythological-religious aspects of Socrates' palinode, it seemed best to preserve the mention of Zeus literally.

229d *the Areopagus*: the 'hill of Ares' just to the west-north-west of the Acropolis where in ancient times the Council used to meet, and where St Paul delivered a famous address.

229e *monstrous natures*: Centaurs were half man, half horse; the Chimaera was a mixture of various creatures; the Gorgon was a snake-haired monstrous female; Pegasus was a winged horse—and Greek mythology was full of such hybrid, impossible creatures.

229e *knowing myself*: somewhere on or near the now-ruined temple of Apollo at Delphi, the main oracular centre for all Greece, was the maxim 'Know yourself.' This maxim was a watchword for Socrates, who believed that philosophy begins and ends with self-investigation and the removal of character flaws, especially the illusory impression of knowledge. There is of course irony in having Socrates here deny that he pays attention to myths, when much of his great second speech on love is mythical in content.

230b *statuettes and figures*: it is typical of the naturalistic bent of Greek folk religion that such a beautiful spot would attract votive offerings of this kind—small figurines representing the appropriate deities.

230d *people in town do*: thus Socrates denies for himself what he will later describe as a kind of divine madness, the inspiration of a seer or prophet (244a–b). For towards the end of the dialogue, at 275b–c, Socrates avows that trees can teach people some things, if their ears are sensitive enough to hear. But here he immediately goes on to acknowledge that Phaedrus can 'charm' or 'enchant' him with the promise of a speech by Lysias, and as the dialogue progresses Socrates often plays with descriptions of himself as sick with love for speeches, or as frenzied as a Bacchant, or possessed by the local deities—as if he had climbed down from his rationalistic pedestal.

Why are we told (here and at *Crito* 52b) that Socrates never leaves town? It is true that this is the only Platonic dialogue where we see Socrates away from his usual urban haunts, but he plainly does leave town, since he is more knowledgeable about the spot than Phaedrus (229b–c). In any case, as Osborne points out ([27], n. 9), it is quite likely that Socrates would have passed by this spot almost daily from his home into town. Is it too far-fetched to suggest that we are having our attention drawn to the crossing of boundaries? The boundary of the city walls (227a) represents the boundary of the vault of heaven, which the philosopher crosses (247b ff.). This analogy is enhanced by the fact that the absolute Beauty knowable in the region beyond heaven corresponds to the natural beauty of the spot by the Ilissus (230b–c). Ferrari calls this episode ([16], p. 18), an 'exemplary little bout' of 'philosophic madness': Socrates' passion, especially in the palinode, is markedly different from his usual rationality. Socrates' knowledge of the countryside outside the city walls also reminds us that he is not as innocent as he is making out: he is pretending to let Phaedrus lead him, when he is actually the leader himself, and over the course of the dialogue will guide Phaedrus to a true conception of rhetoric.

230e *Here I go, then*: there is really no way to tell for sure whether or not the following speech is actually by Lysias, or is a Platonic imitation or parody. I incline towards thinking that it is a parody. The best attempt to argue this case (with references to some earlier work) is by G. E. Dimock, '*Alla* in Lysias and Plato's *Phaedrus*', *American Journal of Philology*, 73 (1952), 381–96. Rowe ([3], pp. 142–3), who believes that it is a genuine speech of Lysias, gives a good summary of the rival issues.

230e *if this were to happen*: a vague phrase for 'if we were to form a relationship'. In the next sentence 'what I want' is an equally vague phrase for 'sex'. This makes the situation of Lysias' speaker odd and incoherent: he claims not to be in love, he equates love with desire, and yet he claims to desire the boy.

231c *such a precious thing*: his chastity or virginity.

232c *what you value most*: as above, chastity or virginity.

233d *other aspirations*: we speak of loving our parents and our friends, and so did the Greeks, but the kind of love at issue throughout the dialogue is *erōs*, which is passionate, and in other contexts may be translated 'lust'. And so it can be distinguished, as in this paragraph, from the gentler kind of affection we feel for parents and friends.

234d *your enthusiasm*: since the speech is so plainly flat, boring, and pedantic, Socrates' irony is particularly marked here. The imagery of enthusiasm (literally, possession by a god) and of ecstasy picks up the mention of Phaedrus' 'frenzy' at 228b. The verbs used both here and at 228b derive from the ecstatic cult of Dionysus. For speech as having magical powers, so that the audience become possessed, see especially Gorgias' fascinating *Encomium of Helen*, a display speech written *c*.425.

235c *the fair Sappho, or Anacreon the wise*: biographical information about Sappho and Anacreon can be found in the Index of Names. It was pointed out by W. W. Fortenbaugh ('Plato, *Phaedrus* 235c3', *Classical Philology*, 61 (1966), 108–9) that mention of these two poets is followed by verbal and thematic allusions to several of their poems in the subsequent speeches of Socrates.

235e *but also of you*: on taking up office, each of the nine archons of Athens—

the administrative magistrates for the year—swore an oath not to violate the laws, and that if he did he would dedicate a golden statue of himself. Plato has Phaedrus combine this reference with one to the famous statue of the orator Gorgias, who set up a (life-sized?) statue of himself at Delphi (the base of which survives in the museum there), not as a punishment, but for glorification. Phaedrus will set up a statue of himself as a penalty, and of Socrates for glorification. Socrates, of course, is the last person to approve of such self-advertisement, and so in the next sentence he pointedly calls Phaedrus 'golden', as if to divert the threat of such a statue away from himself. At 236b Phaedrus makes an even more extravagant offer, since the 'offering of the Cypselids in Olympia' which he mentions was probably a colossal gold statue. For suggestions about these and further resonances, see K. A. Morgan, 'Socrates and Gorgias at Delphi and Olympia: *Phaedrus* 235d6–236b4', *Classical Quarterly*, 44 (1994), 375–86.

236c *pretended he didn't*: Phaedrus has just imitated what Socrates said at 228a and 228c.

236d *hearken well to what I say*: a popular quotation from a lost poem by Pindar (fr. 105 Snell).

237a *cover my head*: why does Socrates cover his head? It seems a peculiarly symbolic action, covering more than just the embarrassment he mentions here. Part of our puzzlement is due to the fact that ancient Greek gestures are not always clear to us. Perhaps it is no more than a device to underscore the importance of the palinode, for which Socrates unveils himself at 243b, or perhaps it is just that Socrates does not want to see Phaedrus' reaction to his speech—does not want to see him enjoying another artificial composition, as he did at 234d. Griswold ([17], p. 55) suggests that it makes Socrates 'a visible icon of his irony'; Calvo (in Rossetti [19]) argues that we are meant to understand his speech as a veiled code, symbolized by Socrates' veiling of his head, so that the speech is not as negative as it seems; for Asmis ([20], p. 162) it symbolizes the fact that Socrates is hiding himself behind an Isocratean kind of speech.

Also, we are plunged into a network of associations, half-glimpsed beneath the surface of the text. Socrates is lying on the ground, listening to Lysias' speech from Phaedrus, which he describes as a *pharmakon* (230d). This word has to be translated 'charm' in this context, but it also means 'drug' or 'medicine', or even 'poison'. It is the word used in *Phaedo* for the hemlock which Socrates takes and which kills him (a cognate word, translated 'bewitched' at 242e, could mean 'poisoned to death'), and in *Phaedo* Socrates covers his head (see 118a), just as in *Phaedrus*, and is lying down. Moreover, the Cypselid offering at Olympia which contemporary readers would first have thought of on hearing the phrase at 236b, just a short while ago, was the coffin-like box in which

Cypselus was hidden as a child by his mother to save him from being assassinated (see the story in Herodotus 5.92). At the very least, then, we might be inclined to say that Socrates' uncovering his head before his palinode represents a kind of resurrection from the emotional death caused by disrespect for Love.

237a *because the Ligurians are so musical*: Plato is indulging in whimsical etymology. 'Clear-voiced', a traditional epithet of the Muses, translates *ligeiai*, so Plato pretends that this could have something to do with the Ligurians, a people who lived on the south coast of modern France (and were not otherwise known as musical). This address to the Muses is modelled on poets' opening prayers for inspiration, and the form 'whether you are this or that' was traditional in Greek prayers, to make sure that you attracted the attention of the deity or deities to whom you were praying by covering all or all the most important attributes.

237a *grant me your support*: the phrase may or may not be an actual quotation from an unknown author, but it is in distinctly poetic language.

237b *that he was not*: Plato has Socrates immediately imagine a situation that is far more plausible than the one in Lysias' speech, where someone who was not in love, and felt no desire, somehow simultaneously did feel desire. However, since, as Halperin [35] stresses, it is part of the definition of what Plato is calling 'love', as opposed to 'desire', that it aims for a specific object, then in aiming for the specific boy who is the target of his speech the non-lover reveals himself really to be a lover. So if we take it that Lysias' speaker was really in love, it follows that he too was pretending, and so Socrates is simply placing his speaker on the same footing as Lysias'. At any rate, there is a clear progression throughout the three speeches, from Lysias' non-lover, to Socrates' secret lover here, to the open lover of his final speech. There is a useful analysis of this second speech, Socrates' first, in M. Brown and J. Coulter, 'The Middle Speech of Plato's *Phaedrus*', *Journal of the History of Philosophy*, 9 (1971), 405–23.

238c *and is called love*: Plato fancifully derives the word *erōs* from the word for 'strength' (*rhōmē*). On this definition of love, see the Introduction, p. xix.

238c *I do*: this interruption to the speech highlights the definition just given, before it is put to work in what follows. It also moves the theme of inspiration and insanity one step further forward.

238c *unusually eloquent, Socrates*: because often in the Socratic dialogues Plato has Socrates display a marked preference for short questions and answers, rather than long speeches: see e.g. *Protagoras* 334c–e, *Gorgias* 449c, 465e–466a, 519d.

238d *possessed by the Nymphs*: we already know from 230b that the location is sacred to the Nymphs. Among their other functions, they were supposed to be able to possess people and drive them crazy, much as we used to say that people could be enchanted by fairies.

238d *chanting dithyrambs*: dithyrambic poetry was a kind of lyric poetry which by the fifth century was notorious for its affected language and florid music.

238d *brave heart*: Plato uses a poetic phrase to parody florid Gorgianic rhetoric.

239b *philosophy*: notice that philosophy is assumed to be a relationship between people. In Socrates' world philosophy was not something you studied from books or even lectures, but something that happened through intimate conversation, as depicted in the Platonic dialogues. See also 274b–278b.

239d *with alien colours and make-up*: there is evidence from elsewhere too that men in ancient Athens used make-up, but it was probably only effeminate men who did so.

240b *a not unrefined kind of pleasure*: the word for 'parasite' also means 'flatterer': a parasite flatters you—hence the 'short-term pleasure'—in order to gain invitations to your dinner table.

240c *youth pleases youth*: the full saying is an unexciting hexameter verse: 'Youth pleases youth, and old age pleases old age.'

241b *at the flip of a sherd*: 'at the flip of a coin', as we would say. Apparently there was a children's game in ancient times in which the choice of which team was 'it' was determined by which way a sherd or a shell fell on the ground.

241b *to chase after him*: i.e. to turn the rules of homoerotic courtship in Greece upside down, since normally the older man chased after the younger boy.

241d *wolves love lambs*: this last sentence is almost a complete line of hexameter verse, and it is tempting to make the slight textual changes required to make it perfect. It is unlikely to be a quotation, but a Platonic composition; and so at 241e Socrates says that he is now uttering epic verse rather than dithyrambs (see 238d)—hexameters being the verse units of epic poetry.

241e *finding fault with things*: the traditional function of epic verse was to sing in praise of the glories of war, so Socrates pretends to feel it inappropriate that he has broken into hexameters when he is doing the opposite of praising. Notice how the stages of Socrates' 'possession by the Nymphs' are marked: he has already moved from the dithyrambic Muse to the epic Muse, but will not be fully possessed until his next speech.

242b *forced others to do so*: in *Symposium* the speeches on Love are delivered at Phaedrus' urging (177a–d), and he himself delivers the first of them.

242c *about to do something*: the most important Platonic passages relevant to Socrates' divine sign are *Apology* 31c–d (to which this passage of

Phaedrus is similar), 40a–b, 41d, *Euthydemus* 272e, *Republic* 496c, *Thea-etetus* 151a. In spurious or possibly spurious Platonic works, the follow-ing two dialogues are important: *Alcibiades I* 103a–b, and especially *Theages* 128d–130e. In Xenophon's Socratic works, the following passages are important: *Apology* 12–13, *Memoirs of Socrates* 1.1.2–5, 4.3.12–13, 4.8.1, 4.8.5–6, 4.8.11, *Symposium* 8.5. We can be sure from all this evidence that it was a genuine trait of the historical Socrates, and it quickly entered the anecdotal tradition and gave rise to many more stories than Plato and Xenophon preserve. For examples, and ancient speculation on the phenomenon, see Plutarch's excellent essay 'On Socrates' Personal Deity'. For modern discussion, see M. Joyal, *The Platonic Theages* (Stuttgart: Franz Steiner, 2000), 65 ff., with his further bibliography. One aspect of the divine sign which our dialogue makes clear is that it occurs randomly (this, of course, is why he calls it 'div-ine'): otherwise it would not have interfered at this late stage, but would have stopped him making the speech in the first place.

242d *in the eyes of the gods*: Ibycus fr. 25 in volume 2 of J. M. Edmonds's Loeb text *Lyra Graeca*.

242d *your speech*: what is the point of this pointed attribution? Socrates goes out of his way to disclaim authorship of the speech. Here, and at 244a and 257b he attributes it to Phaedrus; at 235c he suggests that Anacreon and Sappho contributed to it; at 237a the Muses are invoked for it; and at 238d, 241e, and 263d it is attributed to the Nymphs of the place. Then we note that the first speech, although delivered by Phaedrus, was composed by Lysias, and that even Socrates' great speech, the palinode, is attributed at 244a to Stesichorus rather than Socrates himself. None of the speeches have apparently been spoken by their authors. Night-ingale [64] argues that Plato is stressing the theme of hearsay or 'alien discourse', as opposed to the authentic discourse hinted at in 275a, which comes from within oneself rather than from outside. There are plenty of minor examples of such 'alien discourse' in the dialogue too, making it a true theme: 227a, 257c, 259e–260a, 261b, 266d, 268c, 270c, 271c, 274c. The problem with alien discourse, Nightingale argues, is that its authors are rehashing second-hand material, and that it feeds the baser parts of its recipients' souls. They should cut through the com-plexity of the many Typhonic voices they hear, which threaten to occupy their souls, by focusing only on whether or not what they hear is true. Authentic discourse, by contrast, has been made the author's own as a result of his investigations into truth; is spoken by the author himself, so that he can explain and defend it; and has an educational purpose.

242e *or at least divine*: in *Symposium* 202d–e Love is said not to be a god, but a spirit, intermediate between gods and men. By the same token, he is said there (203b ff.) to be not the son of Aphrodite, but of Plenty and Poverty.

243a *but Stesichorus didn't*: Homer and Stesichorus were both blind. Since blindness was a traditional punishment for offences against the gods, Plato fancifully pretends here that they were blinded because of the false tale they told about Helen. However, Stesichorus, unlike Homer, recognized his offence and recanted in a palinode.

243b *citadel of Troy*: Stesichorus fr. 18 in Edmonds's collection (note on 242d).

244a *the deme Myrrhinous*: a deme was originally a village or district of Attica. Every Athenian citizen belonged to a deme for administrative purposes. In giving Phaedrus his full name, Socrates is aiming for mock solemnity.

244a *from Himera*: since a preserved inscription (*Inscr. Gr.* 14.1213), which probably refers to the poet Stesichorus, says that his father was called Eucleides, Plato is either making a mistake or giving his father the apt name of 'Fair Speaker'. On the attribution of the coming speech to Stesichorus, see the second note to 242d.

244a *False was the tale*: the first line of the Stesichorus fragment quoted at 243a.

244a *Dodona*: Delphi and Dodona were the two chief oracular centres of ancient Greece. At both places, the priestesses went into a trance before uttering their oracles. Plato's assessment of *mantikē* here differs considerably from his low opinion elsewhere (e.g. *Republic* 364b), but as Hackforth says, there is no real contradiction because in these other passages 'Plato was doubtless thinking of a practice which was commonly called *mantikē*, but which he here contrasts with *mantikē* and calls *oiōnistikē*' ([2], p. 58). The difference between the two is the same as the difference between any true art and its merely mechanical forms (268a ff.). Divination through dreams is praised at *Timaeus* 71a–72b, as a way for the gods to communicate with human beings who are otherwise too stupid to be aware of them; and at *Timaeus* 40c–d Plato seems to approve of astrological divination—but this is a controversial interpretation: see my article 'The Evidence for Astrology in Classical Greece', *Culture and Cosmos*, 3.2 (1999), 3–15. The canonical discussion of prophetic and other forms of inspiration in ancient Greece, structured around this passage of *Phaedrus*, is E. R. Dodds, *The Greeks and the Irrational* (Berkeley: University of California Press, 1951), ch. 3, 'The Blessings of Madness'.

244b *the Sibyl*: in Greece a little later than Plato there were several Sibyls—it became the general title for oracular prophetesses—but in his time there was only one, perhaps the one at Cumae near Naples in Italy.

244c *and call it 'prophecy'*: the Greeks were given to fanciful etymologies which were supposed to reveal something of the true nature of the thing itself. The idea is discussed and rejected in *Cratylus*, but in other moods Plato himself could find it significant (see, for instance, *Gorgias* 493a–c).

244d *in the distant past*: examples from legend would be the descendants of

Cadmus in Thebes, and those of Atreus in Argos/Mycenae, though we know of no treatments of these tales which give madness the role Plato assigns it here, unless (as William Ford suggests to me) the madness which possesses the maenads in Euripides' *Bacchae*, so that they kill their own relative Pentheus (a descendant of Cadmus), is a cure of the sickness manifested by his resistance to Dionysus. At any rate, what is clear is that Plato is talking about homoeopathic cure: a kind of religious possession or trance cures a psychological affliction. There is evidence that the type of madness outlined here, which cures inherited curses, was thought to be part of the cult of Orphism, but it is often hard to distinguish Orphic from Dionysian and Corybantic cult. On the whole paragraph, see I. M. Linforth, 'Telestic Madness in Plato, *Phaedrus* 244de', *University of California Publications in Classical Philology* 13 (1944–50), 163–72, and for the general background, see R. Parker, *Miasma: Pollution and Purification in Early Greek Religion* (Oxford: Oxford University Press, 1983), especially pp. 286–317. There may be a connection with the kind of cure adumbrated (but unfortunately no more) by Plato at *Laws* 790d–791b and by Aristotle at *Politics* 1342ª7–11.

245a *from the Muses*: see also *Ion* 533e–534c, *Meno* 99d, *Apology* 22a–c. Socrates' contemporary, the polymath Democritus of Abdera, said, 'Whatever a poet writes when he is possessed and divinely inspired is particularly fine' (fr. 18 Diels/Kranz). Despite what is said in this paragraph about a poet needing madness, skilful poetry is given a more rational basis at 268c–d.

245c *this kind of madness*: however, the analogy between love and the other three recognized kinds of good madness should not be pressed too hard. Love-madness leads to knowledge and, ideally, to an intense mingling of sobriety and insanity, whereas the other three depend on inspiration and are contrasted with sobriety and sanity. All that is common between the four types of madness is that they have positive results and are given to us by the gods. See Rowe [3], 168–71.

245c *the nature of the soul*: some scholars have found the introduction of the soul abrupt, but in a discussion of forms of madness it is perfectly natural. What other seat of madness might there be for an ancient Greek?

245c *Every soul is immortal*: or perhaps 'All soul is immortal.' The argument for the immortality of the soul appears to be similar to what we know (from Aristotle, *On the Soul* 405ª29–b1) of an argument formulated by Alcmaeon of Croton, a thinker of the early fifth century. The Aristotelian passage reads: 'Alcmaeon says that soul is immortal because of its similarity with things that are immortal, a similarity that is based on its being in constant motion. For all the divine bodies—the moon, sun, stars, and the whole vault of heaven—are continuously in motion.' Alcmaeon's argument is teased out by J. Barnes, *The Presocratic*

Philosophers, vol. 1 (London: Routledge & Kegan Paul, 1979), 114–20, and by R. J. Hankinson, *Cause and Explanation in Ancient Greek Thought* (Oxford: Oxford University Press, 1998), 30–3. Other Platonic arguments for the immortality of the soul may be found especially at the end of *Phaedo*, and at *Republic* 608d–611a. Here, though, the argument is (for Plato) unusually terse and taut: 'Plato intends that the argument should convince us by the force of its logic; we are not to take on trust what he says, but to give our assent if and only if we are rationally compelled' (Bett [53], 16). Despite this, though Plato's intention is clear enough, the argument is riddled with unexpressed assumptions, logical twists (if not a fallacy or two), and a topsy-turvy structure in which the conclusion is expressed first and more than one premise is given before the evidence that is supposed to establish it. For discussions, see especially Rowe [3], Robinson [48], Bett [53], Blyth [54], and Hankinson [55]. Essentially, the argument is as follows: 1. What is always in motion is immortal (because anything completely inert is dead). 2. What moves itself is always in motion (as long as it exists). 3. What moves itself is forever in motion, and so is immortal (while something that is other-moved merely has life). 4. Soul is what moves itself. 5. Therefore soul is immortal. It is related to the final argument of *Phaedo*, in that the concepts of soul and of immortality are said to go together as 'cold' and 'snow' do.

245e *principle of soul*: on the idea that only soul is a self-mover, and is therefore responsible for all the movement in the universe, see also *Laws* 893b–899d (in the course of a refutation of atheism). At the beginning of *Physics* VII, Aristotle influentially extended this argument of Plato's to the notion that there is a first cause of movement and change in the universe, which is God. Plato's assumption that the soul is a ceaseless self-mover represents a significant departure from his earlier psychology, as expressed in *Phaedo* and *Republic*, where the soul (or at any rate the essential part of the soul) is changeless.

246a *his team of horses*: the doctrine of the tripartite soul is argued for most famously and fully at *Republic* 434d–441c. It is given a physiological basis at *Timaeus* 69c ff. But even so Plato can talk (as he did at 237d–238c) in a more accessible fashion, using a simple dichotomy between the rational and irrational parts of the soul. It is just that, in fact, the irrational parts are two. It is curious to notice that in Socrates' image the soul, or human self, is hybrid—just as hybrid as Typhon or the other monstrous creatures mentioned at 229d–230a. Though Socrates there denied the value of rationalizing such monsters, he here licenses adopting a psychological interpretation of at least some of them.

246a *are a mixture*: it is significant that even the gods' souls are tripartite. Likewise, at 245c ff., the argument that the soul is immortal and self-moving applies to every soul, divine or human. There is continuity between human and divine souls: they both have the same impulse, to see the Forms. But there are also differences: the gods are untroubled by conflict, and are therefore never incarnated into a physical body. The presence of both horses in the human soul shows that, contrary to many conceptions of the soul in the history of Western thought, Plato does not regard the soul as basically either good or bad. It innately has both good impulses and bad impulses, and it depends on reason—the charioteer—which of the two wins out.

246b *is called 'mortal'*: a question that is made urgent by the doctrine that every living creature has an immortal soul, and is answered by a theory of reincarnation.

246b *all that is inanimate*: throughout his life Plato was convinced, sometimes in a markedly ascetic fashion, of the superiority of the soul to the body, and of mental or psychic goods to physical and external goods. So, for instance, in the early dialogues we are urged to take care of our souls to the virtual exclusion of all else. It is only in his latest dialogue, *Laws*, that Plato fully admits that souls could harm a body (896e), by the lifestyle they chose, for instance.

247a *eleven squadrons*: there were canonical lists of the twelve Olympian gods, but they differed slightly. Given Plato's separation here of Hestia, the goddess of the hearth (perhaps as an image of the earth at the centre of the heavens), he is probably thinking of Zeus, Hera, Hephaestus, Aphrodite, Ares, Poseidon, Demeter, Apollo, Artemis, Athena, Hermes, and Dionysus; these are precisely the twelve familiar to Athenians from the east frieze of the Parthenon. The 'spirits' Plato mentions are probably the various demigods assigned to these major deities (as Eros was Aphrodite's companion, and the Sea-nymphs were Poseidon's), but given what is said at 252c–d they may include the guardian spirits which look after a person in his lifetime and are said in *Republic* to represent the destiny of the incarnation a person has chosen (*Republic* 620d–621a). While the gods in *Phaedrus* appear to retain their traditional Greek roles, they are also astral deities, driving the stars and planets. There is a hint of astral spirits at *Republic* 621b, and the gods reappear as astral deities at *Timaeus* 40a–b and *Laws* 966d–967d.

247a *each performing his proper function*: there is an echo of an important element of *Republic*. In *Republic* 'performing one's own function' is what unifies the ideal city and the human soul, for which the city is an analogy. The gods in *Phaedrus* perform their own function, and they are so unified that it is impossible to distinguish between driver and team of horses.

247b *we call 'immortal'*: strictly speaking, every soul is immortal, but in common parlance we think of only the gods as immortal. It is very unlikely that the spatial imagery in what follows is to be taken literally. This is a controversial aspect of Plato's metaphysics, but although he often speaks of two worlds, the intelligible world and the world of the senses, there is more overlap between them than many scholars have thought. Thus, for instance, in *Phaedrus* as elsewhere, it is the sight of beautiful things in this world that reminds us and sets us in search of absolute Beauty. The 'separation' of the Forms (see next note) is metaphysical difference, not physical separation: they are different in that they are not liable to change and decay, they are immaterial, and so on. But the fact that we do not perceive them is, at least in part, a fault of our perception, not just of their difference (see e.g. 250e).

247e *and returns home*: there can be little doubt that the entities the soul sees in the 'region beyond heaven' are the Forms (as they are usually called), though the religious awe with which they are invested in *Phaedrus* is striking: they alone are what is really real (247c, 249c); they are called 'sacred' (250a), and they occupy a 'holy' place (254b), which is higher even than the gods' home (247e); in fact, the divinity of the gods is somehow due to the Forms (249c), and the gods' minds are fed by the sight of the Forms (247d). This passion alone makes it hard to believe the view of Nehamas (in [4]) that Plato is using the palinode to bid farewell to his middle-period views on Forms.

Here Plato mentions 'justice as it really is', self-control, and knowledge, and describes the domain as a whole as 'true being'. Such a description is standard for the Forms, as is the suffix 'as it really is'; also, the Forms are always immaterial, immutable, and perfect. Though there is argument about the scope of the theory (are there Forms of everything in the world, even beds and chairs, or only of disputable predicates such as beauty?), justice and beauty (250b) are Forms that appear elsewhere in the dialogues, and self-control and knowledge (that is, knowledge of Forms) are comprehensible Forms too, given that here, in typical middle-period mode, Plato is stressing the perfection of Forms, as standards of which their counterparts on earth will inevitably fall short. However, the assumption here that there is a kind of perfect knowledge correlated only with Forms is used at *Parmenides* 133b–134e as the basis of an argument designed to prove that we mortal humans *cannot* have such knowledge. In different contexts in the dialogues, Plato urges us to think of Forms either as perfect standards with pale imitations in the material world, or as entities in which the things of this world partake and which they are named after. The best accounts of Plato's 'theory' of Forms are: A. Wedberg, *Plato's Philosophy of Mathematics* (Stockholm: Almquist & Wiksell, 1955), 26–44; and J. Annas, *An Introduction to Plato's* Republic (Oxford: Oxford University Press, 1981), 190–241. See also the essays collected in vol. 1 of Fine [12] and vol. 2 of Smith [13].

247e *to wash the ambrosia down*: Plato is alluding light-heartedly to Homer, *Iliad* 5.368–9, where the goddess Iris reins in the team of horses she has been lent by Ares and throws them some ambrosia to eat. Blyth ([54], p. 190) may well be right to suggest that this feeding of the horses of the gods' souls is, as it were, the earthing of their souls, so that they have enough connection with physical existence to perform their function of taking care of the world. Note also that this food is the horses' equivalent of the food the gods themselves have been eating in the previous paragraph—the vision of the Forms. By implication, our souls too are nourished by the sight of the Forms (see *Phaedo* 84a–b, *Republic* 490b). The Forms are not just abstract philosophical entities, but a source of life (as are impressions in general: *Republic* 401b–c). We are in the thick of the religious and mystical dimension of Plato's thought, which has been well summarized in the context of this dialogue by K. Seeskin, 'Plato, Mysticism and Madness', *Monist*, 59 (1976), 574–86.

248a *resemble him most*: on the Platonic ideal of 'assimilation to god', see especially *Theaetetus* 172c–177b and *Timaeus* 90b–d, with J. Annas, *Platonic Ethics Old and New* (Ithaca, NY: Cornell University Press, 1999), ch. 3, and D. Sedley, 'The Ideal of Godlikeness', in Fine [12] vol. 2, pp. 309–28.

248b *specious nourishment*: the word translated 'specious' is cognate with *doxa*, which is Plato's usual word for 'opinion', the mental faculty contrasted with knowledge in, especially, *Republic* 507a–518b and 531d–534a.

248b *the plain of truth*: a Pythagorean called Petron of Himera also used this phrase (according to Plutarch, at any rate, in *On the Decline of Oracles* 422b–e), and he is usually thought to have lived before Plato, in which case this may be evidence of Plato's borrowing from Pythagorean tradition. But Petron's dating is uncertain, and Plutarch, as a Platonist, may have embellished his account with this phrase. There are also echoes in what follows of the Presocratic philosopher Empedocles, on which see Hackforth [2], 82.

248d *dedicated to love*: although the Greek reads, literally, 'philosophers or lovers of beauty or men of culture or men who are dedicated to love', it is clear that in no case is the 'or' meant to be disjunctive. A few lines later, at 249a, the same character will be glossed as 'a man who has practised philosophy with sincerity or combined his love for a boy with the practice of philosophy'. Or again, at *Phaedo* 61a Plato has Socrates say that 'the highest music is philosophy' ('men of culture' being literally 'men devoted to the Muses'), and the connection between philosophy (literally 'love of wisdom') and love of beauty is maintained throughout Diotima's speech in *Symposium*, which also shows, as *Phaedrus* does too, how important dedication to love is for a philosopher in the Platonic mould.

These philosophic souls must belong to the second of the three categories of soul described in the previous paragraph. The first category, those who catch a good, even if not quite perfect, glimpse of reality, are not liable to incarnation in this cycle, but the other two categories (those who, almost comically, bob up and down across the frontier of the plain of truth, and those who altogether fail to see reality) are to be incarnated.

Incarnation is a result of ignorance (failure to see the truth), and anything less than complete knowledge of truth is enough to guarantee incarnation.

248e *initiators into one of the mystery cults*: given the mystical tone of this stretch of our dialogue, it may come as a surprise to see how low Plato ranks prophets and initiators. But as *Republic* 364e–365a shows, Plato did not think highly of most such people, who claimed to be able to provide instant fixes for past sins. Redemption, in Plato's view, is a long, hard process.

248e *tyrants*: in *Gorgias* and *Republic* too Plato ranks tyrants as the lowest form of human life. For another list of degenerating incarnations, see *Timaeus* 41d–42d, 90e–92c. At *Phaedo* 81c–82c (as at *Timaeus* 91d–92c) various appropriate animal incarnations are listed. It is an implication of *Phaedrus* 248e and 249b that after one of these nine sorts of first incarnation, a failed soul would be born into the body of an animal; in *Timaeus*, a possible second incarnation, between becoming a man and becoming an animal, is becoming a woman. Plato's belief in reincarnation is most vividly expressed in the myth with which he ends *Republic*.

The ranking here in *Phaedrus* is mysterious, but probably depends on a number of factors: how much knowledge the pursuits involve; what kind of knowledge the pursuits involve; the social value of the pursuits; the political value of the pursuits (on Plato's understanding of political value as determined by ability to see to the true welfare of the citizens); and whether they care for the soul or the body. If I had to summarize all this simply, I would say that the ranking depends on how large the view of the world is for which the person acts as a channel, or in other words how much he is possessed, or in other words (perhaps) how transcendent is the object he loves, or in other words how much control he has over the black horse of his internal chariot, to aid his recollection of the vision of true Beauty he once had.

248e *the opposite*: does this refer to the punishment awaiting them in the underworld between incarnations, or to reincarnation at a different level among the nine ranks just listed? Comparison with *Laws* 903c–905c suggests the latter, though most scholars prefer the former.

248e *ten thousand years*: is the soul at this point necessarily perfect, free from internal conflict, and therefore free from further incarnation? Perhaps not: see R. S. Bluck, 'The *Phaedrus* and Reincarnation', *American Journal of Philology*, 79 (1958), 156–64. Bluck argues that the fall of souls who have failed to catch a glimpse of true reality in the plain of truth is not the original fall; they have been on earth before, and after ten thousand years they simply resume the struggle described at 248a–c to see the truth. But he is decisively refuted by D. D. McGibbon, 'The Fall of the Soul in Plato's *Phaedrus*', *Classical Quarterly*, 14 (1964), 56–63.

249a *they return*: at *Phaedo* 80d–81a, however, philosophers have to undergo only a single incarnation.

249b *in human form*: other myths of afterlife judgement can be found at the end of *Gorgias* and *Republic*. There Plato allows for the possibility that some souls are so wicked that they endure eternal punishment, whereas in *Phaedrus* all souls, however wicked, seem to regain their wings after ten thousand years, or ten incarnations.

249b *the life it likes*: see *Republic* 617d–620d. The brevity of the statement here compared to the fullness of the version in *Republic* strongly suggests that *Phaedrus* was written after *Republic*. But whereas in *Republic* the element of choice was emphasized, here we find a combination between allotment (i.e. by a lottery) and personal choice.

249c *into true reality*: for this theory—the 'theory of recollection'—that recognition of attributes is recollection of pre-incarnate knowledge of Forms, see *Phaedo* 72e–76e. See also *Meno* 80d–86c. The best recent discussion is D. Scott, *Recollection and Experience: Plato's Theory of Learning and Its Successors* (Cambridge: Cambridge University Press, 1995); a more summary version of his views can be found in Fine [12], vol. 1. Plato's argument here is a little obscure, but may be paraphrased as follows: if a soul did not already possess latent knowledge of the singular Forms, it is impossible to conceive how a man could make sense of the variety of sense impressions and group them under single abstract concepts. And so it is unthinkable that a soul could start its existence as an animal, because as an animal it could not have gained the knowledge that enables it to abstract from sense impressions in this way. And so it must have been out on the rim of the universe, and then have been born as a man, before degenerating into animalhood, and then returning to human form.

249d *behaving like a madman*: compare especially the apocryphal story about Thales, an archetypal philosopher, told by Plato at *Theaetetus* 174a–b. Every human soul desires to know Forms, and has an ability to do so. But both the desire and the ability may be overridden by the black horse, unless it is restrained. The philosopher alone has the desire and the ability in full. 'The rapture that marks his success Plato calls "love", and the look of otherworldly devotion in his eyes others call "madness"' (Morgan [26], 177). Plato here compresses the gradual ascent to the Form of Beauty as described in *Symposium* 210a–211c: the various stages of the ascent are implied simply by the assertion that the philosopher 'looks upward'.

249e *anyone who is touched by it*: i.e. especially the lover's beloved: see 255a–256b.

249e *this kind of madness*: Plato may be hazarding an etymology of *erastēs* (lover) from the Greek words for 'love' and 'best'.

250b *we as attendants of Zeus*: we have to wait till 252e to find out that followers of Zeus are philosophers, and so that this is what Plato means here by 'we'.

250c *imprisoned like shellfish*: the last four English sentences translate a single, passionately long sentence in the Greek, which is filled with the terminology of the Eleusinian Mysteries (for a brief account of which see W. Burkert, *Greek Religion* (Oxford: Basil Blackwell, 1985), 285–90). The word translated 'untainted by' could also mean 'unentombed in', and is a reference to the Orphic teaching reflected, for instance, at *Gorgias* 493a, which was neatly captured in Greek in the phrase *sōma sēma*: 'the body is a tomb.'

250c *rather too long now*: an unusual admission from Plato's Socrates that he is one of the initiates, a true philosopher. This is of more than passing interest in context, because at 246a Socrates said that he would produce at best only an image of what the soul is like, and at 273d he says that the best images or likenesses are produced by those who know the truth. As one who knows the truth, then, Socrates is inviting us to regard the myth of the soul as a good likeness.

250d *and especially lovable*: in other words, love of beauty (the experience which is being described as a means to philosophical contemplation) is as close as a human being can get to genuine philosophy (literally, 'love of wisdom'), which is presumably part of the god's divine experience.

251a *unnatural pleasures*: it has been said that this sentence contains a 'contemptuous reference to heterosexual love' and that 'Plato regarded this as deserving of equal condemnation with the unnatural pursuit of pleasure (i.e. a purely carnal homosexual relationship) of which he speaks in the same breath' (Hackforth [2], 98). While it is true that in the second part of the sentence Plato seems to be condemning homosexual intercourse as unnatural, it is not clear that what he is condemning in the first part is heterosexual love in general, rather than the wasting of the energy which is love on the lesser goal of procreation as opposed to the more important goal of attaining immortality (see *Symposium* 208e ff.).

251a *a cult statue or a god*: this seems to be a Greek idiom for being thunderstruck by love: Plato uses it again at *Charmides* 154c. But here in *Phaedrus* the expression gains further overtones, because we know that lover and beloved are followers of the same god. Thus the beloved adumbrates his god just as his beauty adumbrates Beauty. Once the lover has overcome his confusion and lust (253c–255a) the lover sees the beloved as 'godlike' (255a) and the beloved sees that the lover is 'inspired by a god' (255b).

251c *we call it desire*: Plato is hazarding an extremely fanciful etymology, according to which *himeros* ('desire') is derived from the *i* in the Greek word for 'approach', *merē* ('particles'), and *rhein* ('flow').

252b *call him 'Pteros'*: the lines are presumably a Platonic invention, so that half the joke is attributing them to an august figure such as Homer. 'Pteros' is a made-up word, derived from the words for 'winged' and 'love'. They may also be the hint of an obscenity, since *anaptero* (literally 'to flap the wings') can mean 'to excite sexually' (as it does at the end of 255c). The metrical irregularity is that in the first half of the second line a short syllable is treated as short before the consonants *pt*, while in the second half another short syllable is lengthened before the same consonants.

253a *gazing on the god*: two processes are going on at once: the discovery or rediscovery by lovers of their own proper god, and the development of their beloved's discovery or rediscovery. In the case of followers of Zeus, the philosopher's god, this means that in helping others to become philosophers, one develops as a philosopher oneself. The lover's subconscious ('remembered') awareness of his natural god helps him to discover his soul-mate and to develop both his own and his lover's potential.

253a *Bacchant-like*: they are so happy to have found the potential image of their god on earth, in the boy they fall in love with, that they make him as close an image as they can. This not only makes the boy even more like their god, but also brings into consciousness their own awareness of which god they are the servants of. Both these things make them love the boy all the more, which makes them all the more want him to fulfil his Zeus-like potential . . . and so on in a never-ending spiral of increasing love. This behaviour is said to be 'Bacchant-like' because Bacchants infect others with their own enthusiasm for their god, Dionysus.

253b *the same qualities as themselves*: from which it follows that, contrary to hints dropped earlier in the dialogue (e.g. at 248d) and in *Symposium* that the only true lover is a philosopher, others (followers of gods other than Zeus) can also be lovers and therefore philosophers. Plato is clearly talking about twelve different types of human character, which are to be explained as dedication to a particular god: on the possible astrological implications of this, see my article cited in the first note on 244b, at pp. 5–6. For more thoughts on the discrepancy between the idea that only followers of Zeus can be philosophers, and the idea that the followers of any god can be philosophers, see M. Dyson, 'Zeus and Philosophy in the Myth of Plato's *Phaedrus*', *Classical Quarterly*, 32 (1982), 307–11.

253b *dealings with their beloveds*: we already know from 247a that there is no 'meanness' (*phthonos*) among the gods, and from elsewhere in Socrates' palinode that the lover assimilates himself to his god. So there is no meanness in his attitude towards his boyfriend, and this is undoubtedly meant to contrast with the spiteful jealousy which characterized both Lysias' non-lover and the disguised lover of Socrates' first speech. See M. W. Dickie, 'The Place of *Phthonos* in the Argument of Plato's

Phaedrus', in R. M. Rosen and J. Farrell (eds), *Nomodeiktes: Greek Studies in Honor of Martin Ostwald* (Ann Arbor: University of Michigan Press, 1993), 379–96.

253d *the better position*: in a chariot drawn by a pair of horses the more reliable horse was put on the right, the less reliable one on the left.

253d *only by spoken commands*: for a more detailed and less anthropomorphic description of the qualities of a good horse, by a contemporary of Plato, see Xenophon, *On Horsemanship* 1. Plato seems to assume that these horses are male, though in fact it was more usual to use mares for chariot teams. This is because his horses are thinly disguised humans.

254a *the pleasures of sex*: notice that the good horse is here assumed *always* to be an ally of the charioteer, our rational faculty. This effectively makes the soul bipartite rather than tripartite. For more on Plato's psychology, see pp. xix–xx, xxiv–xxvi.

254b *next to self-control*: in the context of talk of memory, images of statues on pedestals are bound to remind one of a common memory technique, which precisely involves picturing qualities as statues, in order to fix them clearly in the memory where they can act as focal points around which to cluster further memories. In ancient and medieval times such memory systems were an important part of the orator's training, so that he could remember whole speeches or declaim on any subject about which he was asked. We know that the statue-imaging system was in use in Roman times, and we know that Socrates' contemporary Hippias of Elis had a memory system, though we do not know what kind it was. On the whole subject, see F. A. Yates, *The Art of Memory* (London: Routledge & Kegan Paul, 1966).

254e *in reverence and awe*: or, as we would say nowadays, his desire has been suppressed or sublimated. Desire has not been transformed, as some commentators think. It is not that the black horse is frightened of the boy, so that lust has been transformed to fear: it fears the punishment it would receive from the charioteer if it sprang lustfully on the boy.

255c *in love with Ganymede*: in de Vries's words ([1], p. 174): 'The fantastic etymology of *himeros*, proposed in 251c, is here playfully sanctioned by attributing it to the god whom philosophers especially are said to follow.'

255d *cannot say where it came from*: it was an ancient Greek folk belief that it was possible to catch ophthalmia just from someone's glance, by a mysterious process similar to that by which a yawn is contagious.

256b *Olympic bouts*: at the Olympic games, a wrestler had to throw his opponent three times to win. Plato uses this as a metaphor for the three lifetimes of philosophy that are required to break out of the wheel of reincarnation (see 249a). The metaphor is suitable since the Olympic games were sacred to Zeus, and so are philosophers, according to Plato;

but he insists that living three lives as a philosopher is even tougher than winning at the real Olympic games.

256c *prestige rather than philosophy*: in this paragraph Plato shows himself to be sympathetic to the second rank of person, the 'timocratic' man of *Republic* 9.

256e *commonly praised as virtue*: on the difference between real and spurious virtue, see especially *Phaedo* 68c–69c.

257a *nine thousand years*: see 248e–249b: 9,000 years is the total time between successive incarnations. What Plato means by a discarnate soul roaming around and under the earth is presumably what is hinted at in *Phaedo* 81c–e, that some souls are so laden with earthy elements that they have to stay near the earth, where they are occasionally visible as ghosts.

257a *insisted on by Phaedrus*: by echoing Phaedrus' words at 234c, Plato has Socrates pretend that it was Phaedrus who insisted on the high-falutin language he used, to surpass the tone of Lysias' speech.

257b *his lover here*: Phaedrus: see 236b and 279b.

257c *so much better constructed than your first one*: see the Introduction (p. xi) for the difference in tone between the first and second parts of the dialogue. Here it remains only to point out that it is Phaedrus who lowers the tone. He makes no comment on the amazing content of the palinode Socrates has just completed, and mentions only its construction. This is part of Plato's characterization of Phaedrus as rather superficial, and as showing more concern to hear speeches—any old speeches—than interest in their content: see 234e, 235b, 235d, 236b, 243b.

257c *as a term of abuse throughout*: presumably because a 'speech-writer' works behind the scenes, and avoids actual involvement in the rough and tumble of public life. There is no way of telling whether this refers to a genuine historical event in Lysias' life.

257d *think badly of them and call them 'sophists'*: Plato was in the process of making the term 'sophist' a term of abuse, instead of meaning just someone who was clever and displayed that cleverness in some way, as a teacher or writer. On the fifth-century sophists, see my *The First Philosophers* (Oxford World's Classics, 2000).

257d *the 'sweet bend', Phaedrus*: the phrase 'sweet bend' was proverbial. Presumably the original bend, which seems to have been in the River Nile, was not sweet at all, but long and dangerous, and so the phrase came to mean glossing something bad as if it were good, or saying one thing while meaning another.

258a *or by both*: the Council and the Assembly were the two main organs of democratic Athens. The Council (of 500 members annually chosen by lot from the ten tribes into which citizens were divided) prepared proposals for presentation to the Assembly, which every male citizen over 18 could attend, if he had the time and inclination.

258b *the theatre*: this is partly a metaphor, prompted by the description of a law-maker as an 'author'. But the theatre of Dionysus was already in occasional use as a meeting-place for democratic assemblies, as it was more regularly later in Athenian history. Note that Plato is making no distinctions at present between the kind of display speeches of which we have had three examples in the dialogue, forensic speeches delivered in a lawcourt, deliberative political speeches, and law-making. He wants to talk about persuasive writing and talking in general. Even verse may be included, as at 258d and *Gorgias* 502c–d.

258c *contemplate his writings*: notice how Plato is parodying elements of the last great speech of Socrates, with talk of immortality, being godlike, and contemplation. The blatant irony supports the interpretation proposed in the Introduction (pp. xxxi–xxxvii) that Plato makes idealized rhetoric an impossible goal. If, *per impossibile*, rhetoricians or politicians such as those mentioned here could attain such a goal, they would be philosophers, and would then truly deserve these epithets.

258e *almost all physical pleasures*: in *Gorgias*, *Republic*, and *Philebus* Plato develops or assumes a 'replenishment' model of pleasure, whereby the feeling of pleasure is only the restoration of a previous pain. Physical pleasures such as eating and drinking are paradigmatic, since hunger or thirst is seen as a pain which is restored when eating or drinking. See J. C. B. Gosling and C. C. W. Taylor, *The Greeks on Pleasure* (Oxford: Oxford University Press, 1982). Here Phaedrus is adopting a philosophical pose, involving contempt for physical pleasures—and implicitly the pleasures of sex above all. Since he is a pleasure-seeker—a devotee of the cheap thrills of rhetoric—it is significant that the only piece of philosophy he is made to spout in the entire dialogue has to do with pleasure: that is all the philosophy he can remember.

259b *seems to have passed me by*: a clear hint that the story that follows is a Platonic invention. This hint is confirmed by the reincarnation element of the story, which would never have been present in a traditional Greek tale. However, it does seem to have been a Greek belief that cicadas were anatomically peculiar: Aristotle says, at *Enquiry into Animals* 532^b, that they have no mouth, eat only dew (which they lap up with a 'tongue-like organ'), and never defecate. At *Symposium* 191c Plato seems to suggest that they have a peculiar sex-life too. Socrates does not, however, directly answer Phaedrus' question: the gift that the cicadas can give us is only gradually revealed over the following pages to be true rhetoric.

259c *they were dead*: more than one recent commentator has found it hard to resist reading this partly as an analogy: we too will be lulled to sleep, like Phaedrus, if we look to speeches only for pleasure, not for edifying content.

97

259d *in the midday heat*: in effect, then, Socrates has prefaced what follows, not with a direct appeal to the Muses (as at 237a), but with an appeal to the cicadas to take a favourable report about them to Calliope and Urania! Notice how we are at midday at the turning-point of the dialogue, and when the dialogue has climaxed with Socrates' fantastic vision of the soul's journeying.

260a *basis for persuasion*: at *Gorgias* 454e–455a, rhetoric is defined as 'an agent of the kind of persuasion which is designed to produce conviction, but not to educate people, about matters of right and wrong'.

260a *not a word to be cast aside*: part of Homer, *Iliad* 2.361.

260e *an unsystematic knack*: Plato is referring, with tongue in cheek, to his own *Gorgias* where, at 462b–465e, he divided arts into branches of expertise and mere knacks, or forms of flattery.

260e *genuinely professional speaking*: the Spartans were famously given to brief and memorable statements. This one may or may not be a Platonic invention; at any rate, something very like it is included in Plutarch's much later collection of Spartan sayings, at *Moralia* 233b.

261a *father of fair children*: see 242a–b, where Phaedrus is said to be responsible for most of the speeches delivered in his lifetime. For the image of fatherhood, see 257b.

261a *leading of the soul*: this phrase translates a single word in Greek, *psychagōgia*, which carries strong connotations of magical allurement. The orator Gorgias described rhetoric as a kind of incantatory force too, in his display speech in defence of Helen of Troy.

261b *Nestor's and Odysseus' handbooks . . . Palamedes' handbook*: for information on these legendary heroes, see the Index of Names. Plato seems to be suggesting that whereas Odysseus and Nestor were famous for public speaking, Palamedes was best known as a private speaker. This is perhaps based on his most famous argument, by which he tricked Odysseus into participating in the Trojan War.

261d *at rest and in motion*: since Plato is plainly summarizing the paradoxical arguments of Zeno of Elea (in southern Italy), then that is who he means by 'the Eleatic Palamedes'. For a recent attempt to argue that Zeno is not the person referred to here, see S. Dušanic, 'Alcidamas of Elaea in Plato's *Phaedrus*', *Classical Quarterly*, 42 (1992), 347–57.

261d *the art of arguing opposite sides of the case*: this whole phrase translates a single word in the Greek, *antilogikē*, which picks up the verb *antilegein* used in 261c and translated 'make opposing speeches'. In an influential book, *The Sophistic Movement* (Cambridge: Cambridge University Press, 1981), G. B. Kerferd argued that *antilogikē* was a technical term describing an argumentative method used by the sophists, 'that of proceeding from a given logos, say the position adopted by an opponent, to the establishment of a contrary or contradictory logos in such a way that the opponent must either accept both logoi, or at least abandon his first position' (p. 63). Clearly, there is little in our present passage to support such a view, and I think A. Nehamas is right to argue against it, in 'Eristic, Antilogic, Sophistic, Dialectic: Plato's Demarcation of Philosophy from Sophistry', *History of Philosophy Quarterly*, 7 (1990), 3–16 (reprinted in his *Virtues of Authenticity: Essays on Plato and Socrates* (Princeton: Princeton University Press, 1999), 108–22).

262d *in the course of his speech*: for the thesis that knowledgeable people make the best liars, see *Hippias Minor*. Which 'two speeches' is Plato referring to? Some think they are (1) Lysias' speech, and (2) Socrates' two speeches taken as one. It is more likely, however, that they are just Socrates' two speeches, as he goes on to acknowledge in the rest of this paragraph. His speeches are examples of speeches delivered by 'someone who knows the truth', while Lysias is an example of someone who doesn't know the truth. It is confusing, but no more, that he then goes on first to criticize Lysias' speech, which is not one of the 'two speeches'. It is only at 265c that he explains in what respect his two speeches 'played with words'—in that they took up opposite positions, moving from censure to praise, although they were spoken by the same person. See especially R. K. Sprague, '*Phaedrus* 262d1', *Mnemosyne*, 31 (1978), 72.

262d *the Muses' representatives*: the cicadas, of course: 259b–d.

263a *and with ourselves*: in *Republic* the existence of disputable qualities is one of the foundations on which the theory of Forms is built: 523a–524d.

264b *an ending*: this is, I think, a rather obscure joke. The word translated 'ending' is the same word translated 'consummation' at 253c.

264d *Here it is*: the epigram also exists in a version with two more lines. The *Palatine Anthology* attributes it to Cleobolus of Lindos (one of the Seven Sages of archaic Greece) or, even less plausibly, to Homer.

265c *from criticism to praise*: here Socrates is plainly treating his two speeches as one, since the first was critical, and the second complimentary.

265d *to explain at any time*: this is presumably a reference to 249b–c, where Socrates said, 'A man must understand the impressions he receives by reference to classes: he draws on the plurality of perceptions to combine them by reasoning into a single class.' The method being recommended as a preliminary to definition is known as the method of collection, whereby apparently disparate things are seen to belong to a single genus. Socrates immediately goes on to suggest that his definition of love illustrated the procedure: at 237d ff. love was 'collected' under the genus 'desire', and then further under the kind of desire which is excessive, and this led to his definition of love at 238b–c. The second method, seen as a corollary to collection, is division, whereby the genus is cut up again until the term that is to be defined is reached. Socrates suggests in 265e–266a that both of his two speeches made use of the process of division to distinguish the different kinds of madness, bad and good (see the first note on 266b). At 266b Plato has Socrates say that he is enamoured of these processes, and it is true that collection and division, especially the latter, were frequently used and commended by Plato in some of his later dialogues, notably *Philebus*, *Sophist*, and *Statesman*. In *Sophist* they are given metaphysical backing, too. On the whole topic, see, for instance, J. L. Ackrill, 'In Defence of Platonic Division', in id., *Essays on Plato and Aristotle* (Oxford: Oxford University Press, 1997), 93–109; A. C. Lloyd, 'Plato's Description of Division', in R. E. Allen (ed.), *Studies in Plato's Metaphysics* (London: Routledge & Kegan Paul, 1965), 219–30; J. M. E. Moravcsik, 'The Anatomy of Plato's Divisions', in E. N. Lee *et al.* (eds), *Exegesis and Argument: Studies in Greek Philosophy Presented to Gregory Vlastos* (Assen: Van Gorcum, 1973), 324–48; J. R. Trevaskis, 'Division and Its Relation to Dialectic and Ontology in Plato', *Phronesis*, 12 (1967), 118–29.

265e *as an incompetent butcher might*: the importance of natural divisions is discussed especially at *Statesman* 262a–263a.

266a *on the left hand*: the Greek word is also a term of abuse, covering a range from 'awkward' to 'crass' or 'coarse'. If Socrates' first speech covered base love, and his second speech noble love, one might be justified in wondering whether there is a broader conception of love which unites the two. Such a wider conception may be implicit in the palinode, but has already been given more clearly in *Symposium*, where love is seen as the motivating energy behind whatever one does, since in everything we aim for the good, and the good is the proper aim of love.

266b *that come our way*: the division of the first speech is as follows:

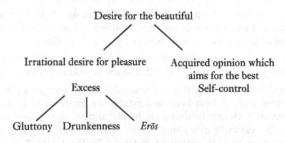

And the division of the second speech is as follows:

266b *as if he were a god*: an adaptation of a Homeric formula which occurs at several places in *Odyssey*: 2.406, 3.30, 5.193, 7.38.

266c *dialecticians*: 'dialectic' is Plato's constant term for his philosophical method. It is related, etymologically, with the Greek word for 'conversation', because (as portrayed in Plato's earliest dialogues) his mentor, Socrates, practised philosophy through talking to other people. In Plato's middle period dialectic took on a more metaphysical and mystical hue, and in his final period it is most commonly used for this method of collection and division. However, there are grounds for thinking that Plato saw more similarities than differences between these different phases of dialectic: see K. Sayre, *Plato's Analytic Method* (Chicago: University of Chicago Press, 1969).

266c *as if they were royalty*: one of Plato's commonest slurs against the sophists was that they taught for money. This was one of the ways in which he distinguished them from Socrates.

266e *arguments from probability*: Socrates' list confuses parts of a speech with types of argument. One might have thought that Plato would have taken more interest in the latter, at any rate. 'But . . . his hostility here is directed not so much at the particular items, techniques of argument or otherwise, that Socrates ticks off, but at the very fact that Socrates is able to tick them off in this fashion. What he objects to is this: that since these rhetorical "Arts" are no more than collections of useful precepts and devices, a student could learn how they are useful without learning how to use them' (Ferrari [16], 70–1). This connects with the criticism of writing at the end of the dialogue, 274c–275e. Here, however, all that is said is that one must not rely on rules alone: natural ability, knowledge, and practice are all necessary too (269d).

267c *the mighty Chalcedonian*: Thrasymachus (see the Index of Names).

268e *not music itself*: some scholars take this as evidence for Plato's denigration of the practical aspects of any science or branch of expertise, as if he were saying here that the ability to play the lyre was insignificant compared to the rarefied theoretical aspects of the discipline. This is probably reading too much into the passage, which may simply be comparing basic with technical ability at any level. On the whole controversy concerning Plato's alleged denigration of science, especially in *Republic*, see A. Gregory, *Plato's Philosophy of Science* (London: Duckworth, 2000).

269a *honey-tongued Adrastus*: a reminiscence of half a line from the seventh-century Spartan poet Tyrtaeus. After the pairing of Euripides and Sophocles, and of Acumenus and Eryximachus, it seems likely that the reference is to another contemporary Athenian statesman, along with Pericles, but if so we cannot identify him.

269e *my friend*: Pericles comes under heavy attack in *Gorgias* 515e ff. as a statesman, and this compliment to him here as an orator is undermined by the palpable irony of the passage. In any case, even if he went about things in the right way, he wasted the effort on rhetoric rather than philosophy, and (since he gained his lofty perspective from Anaxagoras, who is taken to task by Plato at *Phaedo* 97b–99d) he based his approach on the wrong kind of philosophy.

270a *with one's head in the clouds*: this was the popular view of natural science, and hence of philosophy in general. Plato here defiantly turns the phrase against the detractors of philosophy.

270c *the nature of the whole*: it is tempting to understand this as 'the nature of the universe', and to think that Plato is adumbrating some kind of view whereby the soul is a microcosm of the macrocosmic universe. But the lack of any further reference to the universe suggests otherwise, as does the immediately following reference to Hippocrates. Hippocrates was a bit of a reductionist: he would not have referred to the universe as a model of the body (though this may beg the question, since we lack certain knowledge of what Hippocrates himself thought, and this is an early reference to him). More plausibly, Plato is attributing to Hippocrates (not, apparently, on the basis of anything in any of the extant Hippocratic treatises) the view that one will never understand any part of the body well enough without understanding the body as a whole. Likewise, then, he is saying that we will not understand the working of the soul in any respect unless we understand the soul as a whole. For discussions and various views, see H. Herter, 'The Problematic Mention of Hippocrates in Plato's *Phaedrus*', *Illinois Classical Studies*, 1 (1976), 22–42; J. Mansfeld, 'Plato and the Method of Hippocrates', *Greek, Roman, and Byzantine Studies*, 21 (1980), 341–62; D. Tsekourakis, 'Plato's *Phaedrus* and the Holistic Viewpoint in Hippocrates' Therapeutics', *Bulletin of the Institute of Classical Studies*, 38 (1991–3), 162–73.

271c *the actual words*: that is, Socrates doesn't want to write a rhetorical manual himself.

272c *as the saying goes*: in an imagined dispute between a wolf and some shepherds, both sides of the case should be heard.

272d *at the beginning of this discussion*: 259e–260a. This is also the passage Phaedrus refers to at 273a, because the point that orators use arguments from probability is obviously related to the point that they appeal to the opinions of the masses.

273c *whatever he likes to be called after*: Tisias' teacher was Corax, whose name means 'crow'.

273d *not long ago*: 261e–262b.

274a *not the trivial ones you suppose*: that is, mere success in the lawcourts and so on.

274b *what makes it undesirable*: see 257d, where this question was left hanging.

274c *The story I heard*: actually, the story is another Platonic invention: see 275b. He sets it in Egypt because the Egyptians were famous for their records of the ancient past, as Herodotus stresses in the second book of his *Histories* and as Plato himself says at *Timaeus* 22a–b and 23a. Naucratis was a Greek trading station in Egypt, established in the sixth century according to Herodotus (2.178–9), but pottery finds date its establishment to late in the previous century (for a good summary of Greek activity there, see J. Boardman, *The Greeks Overseas* (Harmondsworth: Penguin, 1964), 133–69). For the implications of the story—especially the doubt cast on the value of writing— see the Introduction, pp. xxxvii–xlii. For the echoes in it of the Greek Palamedes story, see Nightingale [64], 149–54; and for the echoes it contains of contemporary debate on the value of written as opposed to off-the-cuff speeches, see Hackforth [2], 162.

274d *Egyptian Thebes*: to distinguish it from the main city of Boeotia on the Greek mainland, which had (and still has) the same name.

275a *atrophy people's memories*: it is perhaps worth remembering how at the start of the dialogue (228d) Phaedrus was embarrassed to have borrowed a copy of Lysias' speech in order to memorize it. In fact, he deliberately borrowed the speech from its author, and so preferred the dead words of the written speech to the possibility of dialogue with the author. In the rest of the dialogue, he has been treated to undigested, spontaneous, unwritten words from a teacher, which at least gives him the chance of receiving knowledge. Plato makes similar remarks about the inability to talk to a book at *Protagoras* 329a and *Theaetetus* 164e, and at *Statesman* 294a ff. he points out the limitations of written-down laws along the same lines.

275a *their own inner resources*: a clear indication that Thamous' worry is that recollection in the technical Platonic sense of recollection of Forms, or the region beyond the heavens (247c ff.), will atrophy in favour of ordinary memory. 'The distinction at issue is not between someone who remembers everything he sees and hears . . . and someone whose memory is so bad that he has to keep looking everything up to refresh it. Thamus is worried about people whose memories are full, not empty— but full of "book knowledge" ' (Griswold [17], 206).

275b *spoken by an oak*: in a trance, the priestesses would interpret the rustling of the leaves of an oak tree.

275b *oak and rock*: this was a proverbial pairing, representing anything dense and insensitive.

275d *an aloof silence*: one might also add that the written word ignores all the unspoken aspects such as body language, tone of voice, and so on, which constitute a major proportion of communication.

275e *defending or helping itself*: the metaphor of speech 'defending itself' recurs several times, at 276a, 276c, 277a, and 278c. It means that written speech cannot, and living dialectical conversation can, respond to questions. The form or forms such response might take is not made clear, but presumably include (1) restating the case in other, clearer terms, and (2) justification by means of alternative arguments.

276a *a mere image of this*: it is a little surprising that Phaedrus is made to appreciate this and come up with the idea himself. I think he knows that Socrates' words are like this. To see Socrates as a 'sensible farmer' of words, to use the image that immediately follows in 276b, is no more than to see him as a midwife, as at *Theaetetus* 149a ff.

276b *gardens of Adonis*: for Adonis, see the Index of Names. 'Gardens of Adonis' were pots in which plants were forced to mature in time for his festival, when they would wither and die in the midsummer sun to represent the death of Adonis, or the passing of youth.

276c *who knows about right and fine and good activities*: more literally, 'who has pieces of knowledge about right things, fine things, and good things'. Some commentators (e.g. Rowe [3], ad loc.) stress the plural 'pieces of knowledge', and argue that Plato is showing himself now to be sceptical about the possibility of attaining overarching knowledge. However, overarching knowledge is exactly what the scientific orator is supposed to have (e.g. 273d–e), so it is hard to argue that Plato has given this up as an ideal. In my translation, I assume that the plural 'pieces of knowledge' is due to infection by the plural 'right and fine and good activities'.

276c *in black water*: to write in or on water was proverbially futile. 'Black water' is of course ink.

276d *age of forgetfulness*: the words scan as half a hexameter, but if they are a quotation, the original source cannot be identified.

277c *a simple speech*: every soul is complex, in that it contains three parts, but at 230a a soul was described as 'simple' if it had tamed its appetitive impulses. It is simple in the sense that the three parts are unified under the rule of reason.

277e *rhapsodes*: professional reciters of poetry, especially the Homeric epics, and lecturers on the topic. Plato's *Ion* contains a devastating character sketch of one.

278c *a title derived from these pursuits*: that is, he should not be called a 'speech-writer', for instance, which Phaedrus said at 257c was used as a term of abuse.

278d *lover of wisdom*: in Greek, *philosophos*—a philosopher.

278e *The beautiful Isocrates*: the reference to Isocrates is not quite unique, since (although not mentioned by name) he is the target of similar criticism at the end of *Euthydemus*—as not quite committing himself to what Plato saw as philosophy. It is possible that an astute reader would not have been surprised at this mention, since the dialogue has contained a number of echoes of and allusions to his work (see de Vries [1], 16, and Asmis [20]). There can be little doubt that there was rivalry between the two contemporary teachers, and that 'it was Plato's intention to wound someone he found vain and tiresome through a complex of allusions that were unmistakably hostile in their connotations and clearly designed to hurt' (Coulter (reference below), 226). Above all, Plato taunts Isocrates with his use of the word *philosophia*: this is the word Isocrates used for what he taught, but by the time *Phaedrus* was written, he was 70-odd years old, and was hardly going to turn to what Plato called *philosophia*, as Plato here suggests he might have done in his youth, at the dramatic date of the dialogue. For this and further details, see R. L. Howland, 'The Attack on Isocrates in the *Phaedrus*', *Classical Quarterly*, 31 (1937), 151–9; G. J. de Vries, 'Isocrates' Reaction to the *Phaedrus*', *Mnemosyne*, 6 (1953), 39–45; J. A. Coulter, '*Phaedrus* 279a: The Praise of Isocrates', *Greek, Roman, and Byzantine Studies*, 8 (1967), 225–36; Morgan [59], 182–7. The contrary view, that Plato's words are sincere and complimentary, is taken by, among others, Hackforth ([2], especially pp. 166–7, but use his index to track further references). The importance of the rivalry between Plato and Isocrates is brilliantly discussed in the first chapter of Nightingale [64], and see also pp. 139–42 of her book.

279c *This prayer will do for me*: the prayer is subjected to detailed analysis by T. G. Rosenmeyer, 'Plato's Prayer to Pan (*Phaedrus* 279b8–c3)', *Hermes*, 90 (1962), 34–44, and by D. Clay, 'Socrates' Prayer to Pan', in G. W. Bowersock *et al.* (eds), *Arktouros: Hellenic Studies Presented to Bernard M. W. Knox* (Berlin: de Gruyter, 1979), 345–53. Different types of prayer in Plato's dialogues are classified and analysed in B. D. Jackson, 'The Prayers of Socrates', *Phronesis*, 16 (1971), 14–37.

279c *friends share everything*: a proverb quite often quoted by Plato: *Lysis* 207c; *Republic* 424a, 449c; *Laws* 739c.

TEXTUAL NOTES

229e1: I read πλήθει καὶ ἀτοπίᾳ with Athenaeus, Pap. Oxyr. 1016 and the second hand of Paris 1811.

234a8: I read παυσαμένης τῆς ὥρας with Ast (and some minor MSS).

235a2: I see no need for the added ἄν

236c3: Punctuating with a full stop after ἀλλήλοις and then retaining εὐλαβήθητι with Viljoen.

244c5: I delete the comma after ἐμφρόνων.

245c8: I replace the comma of the OCT with a full stop, following de Vries and Rowe.

245e1: Reading γένεσιν with the MSS and others.

248d6: I delete the ἤ proposed by Badham and accepted by the OCT.

249b7: Reading δεχόμενον with Platt.

250d6: I punctuate with a comma rather than a dash after ἰόν.

252d5: Reading ἔρωτα without an initial capital (see de Vries).

253c3: Reading τελευτή with the majority of the sources.

255c7: With a comma after ἰέναι.

255d2: Omitting τε with Beare.

257d9–e1: Omitting ὅτι ἀπὸ τοῦ μακροῦ ἀγκῶνος τοῦ κατὰ Νεῖλον ἐκλήθη as an obvious gloss, with Heindorf originally, and several editors since.

258a1–2: Reading συγγράμματος with Heindorf.

263b6: Reading τέχνη with Solmsen.

263c1: Omitting εἶδος with Richards.

267a4: Reading a question mark after παρεπαίνους, as suggested by de Vries.

268a2: Reading καί ποτ' with de Vries and many editors.

270a5: Retaining ἀνοίας with the MSS.

272b3: Retaining the MSS reading οὕτως ἤ ἄλλως.

274d4: Reading Θαμοῦν instead of θεόν, with Postgate.

279a4: Omitting λόγους with Platt.

INDEX OF NAMES

For further information, see the *Oxford Classical Dictionary*, 3rd edition, edited by S. Hornblower and A. Spawforth.

Achelous: the god of rivers, and so often accompanied by Nymphs, who are minor deities associated with natural phenomena. At 263d the Nymphs are even said to be his daughters.

Acumenus: a doctor who is mentioned several times in Plato's dialogues. His son, Eryximachus, also a doctor, is one of the characters and speech-givers of Plato's *Symposium*.

Adonis: a beautiful legendary youth of eastern origin, who was loved by both Aphrodite and Persephone. Zeus decreed that he should spend four months of the year in the underworld with Persephone, four months in the upper world with Aphrodite, and four months doing whatever he chose.

Adrastus: legendary king of Argos or Sicyon, who led the ill-fated expedition of the Seven against Thebes.

Anacreon: sixth-century lyric poet from Teos, especially famous for his love poems.

Anaxagoras: fifth-century 'Presocratic' philosopher of considerable sophistication. Though born in Clazomenae, he spent much of his life in Athens, where he was a close friend of Pericles. Plato's mention at 270a of Anaxagoras' talk of 'mind' is a reference to his attribution to a cosmic mind or intelligence of the original cosmogonic motion.

Aphrodite: goddess of love, beauty, and sexual passion. She is often portrayed as being accompanied by her son, Eros or Love personified (who became debased as the chubby winged Cupid of Roman and later times).

Apollo: the god of culture, music, disease, healing, the sun, and prophecy.

Ares: the god of war and especially of the frenzy of war.

Boreas: the north wind personified. For the story alluded to at 229b, see under OREITHUIA.

Cephalus: originally from Syracuse, the wealthy Cephalus had long been resident in Piraeus. His house is the setting for Plato's *Republic*, in which he plays a small part as one of Socrates' interlocutors in the first book. His most famous child was Lysias, the speech-writer who features in *Phaedrus*.

Cypselids: literally, 'descendants of Cypselus', i.e. Periander and Psammetichus, who followed Cypselus as tyrants of Corinth in the seventh century.

Darius: Darius I, king of Persia 521–486, effectively reconstituted the Persian Empire (see Herodotus 3.89–97), and so Plato counts him at 258b–c among law-givers such as Solon and Lycurgus.

Dionysus: the god of emotional release, whether that comes from mystic ecstasy or from drunkenness.

Epicrates: nothing is known about this man, except that he had a splendid beard!

Eryximachus: see ACUMENUS.

Euripides: c.485–406, with Aeschylus and Sophocles, one of the three geniuses of classical Athenian drama.

Evenus: a fifth-century sophist, originally from the island of Paros, about whom very little is known. He was a poet as well as a teacher of rhetoric.

Ganymede: a good-looking legendary prince of Troy with whom Zeus fell in love. In his only act of homosexual seduction (compared to his many heterosexual affairs), Zeus took him away to Olympus to act as cup-bearer to the gods.

Gorgias: c.480–376, from Leontini in Sicily; one of the giants of the fifth-century sophistic movement, and a well-known figure in Athens. As well as philosophy, he specialized in rhetoric, in which he was a great innovator. Although much of his style nowadays seems—and seemed so even a generation or two after his time—florid and artificial, it apparently dazzled his contemporaries. In the dialogue *Gorgias* Plato uses him as a representative of amoral rhetoric.

Helen: Helen, the most beautiful woman in the world, was married to Menelaus of Sparta, but ran off with Paris to Troy and so initiated the Trojan War, the subject of Homer's *Iliad*. Although Homer's portrait of her is very human, she was the daughter of Zeus, and was worshipped at Sparta and elsewhere.

Hera: Zeus' wife, and goddess of marriage. Her royal qualities are constantly stressed in myth, portrait, and poetry: this is the background of her function at 253b.

Hermes: god of communication, heralds, magic, and wayfarers. If the common thread to these functions is that Hermes crosses boundaries (and returns with information from elsewhere), *Phaedrus* is a peculiarly Hermetic dialogue: see note to 230d.

Herodicus: a doctor, originally from Megara but resident in Selymbria in Thrace, whose devotion to regimen is mocked by Plato at *Republic* 406a–b.

Hestia: the goddess of the hearth and home.

Hippias: from Elis, one of the great sophists of the end of the fifth century, especially famous as a polymath who claimed to be able to answer any question that was put to him.

Hippocrates: the famous fifth-century doctor and medical theorist from the island of Cos. To call him an 'Asclepiad' (270c) is just to say that he is a doctor, a devotee of the healer-god Asclepius. Hippocrates was regarded by his immediate followers and ever since as the founder of scientific medicine, as distinct from folk healing.

Homer: the earliest and greatest of the epic poets, who wrote the *Iliad* and *Odyssey* (if they are by the same hand) c.700 BCE.

Phaedrus: *c*.450–390, Phaedrus is mentioned briefly in Plato's *Protagoras*, but figures prominently in *Symposium*, where he gives the first speech about love. He was exiled from Athens in 415, when he was caught up in the scandal, which also brought down Alcibiades, surrounding the mutilation of the Herms just before the vast Athenian expedition set sail for Sicily. Herms were busts of Hermes on top of square-cut blocks of stone, set up at road junctions in Athens. They had erect phalluses, and on one night they all had their phalluses broken off, and were otherwise mutilated. Phaedrus returned to Athens after the end of the war, when a general amnesty was declared.

Pharmaceia: a playmate of Oreithuia. Intriguingly, given the context of her mention at 229c, her name means 'Scapegoat'.

Pindar: 518–*c*.440, from Cynoscephalae in Boeotia, the most famous lyric poet of ancient Greece. Quite a few of his poems survive, particularly those celebrating athletic victories.

Polemarchus: see LYSIAS.

Polus: from Acragas in Sicily, a pupil of Gorgias, and an imitator of his rhetorical techniques. He is one of the interlocutors in Plato's *Gorgias*.

Prodicus: originally from the island of Ceos, one of the giants of the sophistic movement of the later fifth century. He was especially famous for his work towards what was, in effect, the first Greek dictionary, by defining terms and especially near-synonyms, but we also have extant a paraphrase of a moral story he wrote, in which the hero Heracles, when young, has to choose between a life of virtue or one of vice.

Protagoras: from Abdera in northern Greece, the first and greatest of the sophists. His ideas are extensively reflected in Plato's *Protagoras* and *Theaetetus*. He was a relativist, a democratic theorist, a teacher of rhetoric (especially how to argue both sides of a case), and an agnostic.

Sappho: lyric poetess from Lesbos, living in the late seventh and early sixth centuries. Because she addressed some of her love poems to young women, homoerotic love between women is called 'lesbian'.

Simmias: despite being a Theban, which would have made travel to Athens during the war years more or less impossible, Simmias appears to have been a follower of Socrates, and in *Phaedo* Plato has him present on Socrates' last day alive. It is not clear from what little we know of the man why Plato presents him at 242b as a particular devotee of speeches.

Sirens: mythical enchantresses who attempted, by means of their singing, to lure voyagers such as Odysseus and Orpheus to their deaths.

Socrates: 479–399, the constant protagonist of Plato's early and middle-period dialogues. Historically, he came from a wealthy middle-class family, but he ignored business in favour of philosophy; hence in this dialogue he is poor and goes barefoot. Despite being, probably, a late-middle-period dialogue, *Phaedrus* continues the characterization of Socrates which is prominent in earlier dialogues. He is sharp (and could on occasion be savagely so), enjoys banter with his young friends, has a profound commitment to what he sees as the truth, sees philosophy as a way of improving one's life, declares his own ignorance, and so on.

Solon: *fl. c.*590, a famous Athenian statesman and lyric poet. He is one of the constant members of the varying lists of the Seven Sages of Greece, and was regarded in Athenian popular history as the founding father of their democracy.

Sophocles: *c.*495–406, with Aeschylus and Euripides, one of the three geniuses of classical Athenian drama.

Stesichorus: a lyric poet active early in the sixth century BCE. Little is known of his life, but Plato says at 244a that he came from Himera, on the north coast of Sicily. He was famous for his vivid embellishments of myth and legend. When he became blind after composing a poem which insulted Helen by claiming that she had run off to Troy with Paris, he composed his famous palinode, saying that she was innocent of causing the Trojan War—that she never left home, and that Paris eloped with her mere apparition. Since we have few fragments of Stesichorus' work, the story survives best through Euripides' *Helen*.

Thamous: not the name of any known Egyptian king, and perhaps a corruption of 'Amous', or Amon (Amun), the god who became identified with Ra, the Sun-god, and became the chief deity of Egypt.

Theodorus: of Byzantium, a fifth-century orator about whom we know very little.

Theuth: better known as Thoth (or Tahuti), the ibis-headed Egyptian equivalent to the god Hermes, in his capacity as god of scribes and communication. Plato perhaps uses the name 'Theuth' to remind his readers of the end of the Greek name 'Prometheus', because Prometheus was the inventor of writing in Greek myth.

Thrasymachus: of Chalcedon, famous in his day (the late fifth century) as a superb orator, with clear diction and striking phraseology, but very little of his work in this sphere has survived—just the odd phrase and one fragment. So he is more famous today as Socrates' amoral opponent in the first book of *Republic*.

Tisias: from Syracuse in Sicily, said (along with Corax) to have been the original developer of rhetorical techniques. He was probably working in the early to middle of the fifth century. He may have worked on judicial oratory, while Corax worked on deliberative speech-making; both of them almost certainly began to distinguish the stages of a properly constructed speech, perhaps demarcating preamble, exposition, proof, and conclusion. They both also stressed the importance of arguments from probability.

Typhon: a monstrous creature with 100 snake-heads and fire-blazing eyes, who was defeated by Zeus in his quest for control of the world, and imprisoned in Tartarus, but is still responsible for storms on the earth.

Zeus: king of the gods. As the most elevated of the gods, he is taken by Plato to be the appropriate god for philosophers.

MORE ABOUT **OXFORD WORLD'S CLASSICS**

The Oxford World's Classics Website

www.worldsclassics.co.uk

- Browse the full range of Oxford World's Classics online

- Sign up for our monthly e-alert to receive information on new titles

- Read extracts from the Introductions

- Listen to our editors and translators talk about the world's greatest literature with our Oxford World's Classics audio guides

- Join the conversation, follow us on Twitter at OWC_Oxford

- Teachers and lecturers can order inspection copies quickly and simply via our website

www.worldsclassics.co.uk

American Literature

British and Irish Literature

Children's Literature

Classics and Ancient Literature

Colonial Literature

Eastern Literature

European Literature

Gothic Literature

History

Medieval Literature

Oxford English Drama

Poetry

Philosophy

Politics

Religion

The Oxford Shakespeare

A complete list of Oxford World's Classics, including Authors in Context, Oxford English Drama, and the Oxford Shakespeare, is available in the UK from the Marketing Services Department, Oxford University Press, Great Clarendon Street, Oxford OX2 6DP, or visit the website at www.oup.com/uk/worldsclassics.

In the USA, visit www.oup.com/us/owc for a complete title list.

Oxford World's Classics are available from all good bookshops. In case of difficulty, customers in the UK should contact Oxford University Press Bookshop, 116 High Street, Oxford OX1 4BR.

A SELECTION OF   **OXFORD WORLD'S CLASSICS**

Bhagavad Gita

The Bible Authorized King James Version
With Apocrypha

Dhammapada

Dharmasūtras

The Koran

The Pañcatantra

The Sauptikaparvan (from the
    Mahabharata)

The Tale of Sinuhe and Other Ancient
    Egyptian Poems

Upaniṣads

ANSELM OF CANTERBURY   The Major Works

THOMAS AQUINAS   Selected Philosophical Writings

AUGUSTINE   The Confessions
    On Christian Teaching

BEDE   The Ecclesiastical History

CANDRA   The Lives of the Jain Elders

The Recognition of Śakuntalā

Madhumalati

The Bodhicaryāvatāra